This book is written for our children to help explain
all the moves we made while they were growing up.

I have lived on this farm for almost fifty-two years. I raised Australian shepherds for forty years.

My husband, Carl, always said, "When it's my time to go and the Lord comes to get me, I want to be working on my farm." That's exactly what happened. On December 30, 2006, Carl came in for lunch. I kissed him as he went back outside. When he didn't return at dinnertime, I called our son Eugene. We went looking for Carl. I found his body. He had died of a brain aneurysm while working on his farm. We had been married fifty-five years, twenty-nine days, and approximately five hours. I would do it over again in a heartbeat.

Our oldest son, Steven, graduated from West Virginia Technical College in Montgomery, West Virginia, in 1970 with honors. Steven was an electrical engineer and was hired by the United States Navy before his graduation. He worked at Dahlgren Naval Station and lived in Colonial Beach, Virginia. He passed away on February 2, 2006, from colon cancer. He would have retired in July of that year.

Our son Richard graduated from West Virginia Technical College in Montgomery, West Virginia, in 1972 with honors. Richard was a mechanical engineer. He was also hired by the United States Navy before his graduation and also worked at Dahlgren Naval Station and lives near Fredericksburg, Virginia. He retired in July 2009.

Our son Eugene, after graduating from Hinton High School in 1973, attended Auto-Diesel College in Nashville, Tennessee. When he retired in 2019, he was the manager of the Walker Machinery Company in Sophia, West Virginia. Eugene has lived on the farm for the last twenty-five years. They built a beautiful new home.

Ronda graduated valedictorian from Hinton High School in 1976 and graduated from Fairmont State College. She now works in the office at Ruby Memorial Hospital in Morgantown, West Virginia.

We have six grandchildren. Great-grandchild number 12 is due in November.

Loretta Amick

Mom!
THE MOVERS
ARE HERE

LORETTA AMICK

NEWMAN SPRINGS PUBLISHING
320 Broad Street
Red Bank, NJ 07701

First originally published by Newman Springs Publishing 2022

ISBN 978-1-63881-469-6 (Paperback)
ISBN 978-1-63881-470-2 (Digital)

Printed in the United States of America

"**M**om! The movers are here" was a phrase I heard often but not so much in the beginning. So let's go back to the beginning.

Carl William Amick was born on January 31, 1930. He was born at home in Hickory Flats, just south of Nutterville in northern Greenbrier County, West Virginia. His parents were William Bartlett Amick and Lena Florence Nutter. He joined his three older brothers: Fred was born in 1922, Ray was born in 1924, and Robert was born in 1926. In 1939, his little sister, Laura May, was born with cerebral palsy. Carl's father, Bartlett, was a farmer. He also carried the mail and did his share of time on the fire tower behind Sugar Grove Church. Carl's mother, Lena, had been a schoolteacher before she married. Carl attended the one-room school across the line in Nicholas County. He had to walk about a mile. Everyone in the little one-room school was kin to him. His mother was one of seventeen children.

By the time Carl graduated from eighth grade, his brothers had all left home. His oldest brother, Fred, after graduating from high school, had gotten a job at the King Cole Hotel in Rainelle, West Virginia. One day, a representative from Auto-Diesel College in Nashville, Tennessee, was staying at the hotel. After talking with the representative, Fred decided to go to Nashville and attend Auto-Diesel College. After graduating from the college, Fred moved to Burbank, California, and worked for Lockheed. Fred married Jane, a California girl. When Ray graduated from high school, he joined the navy. After boot camp, he was sent to Oakland, California. After World War II was over, Ray returned to Oakland and opened a welding shop and married Georgia, another California girl. Robert did not finish high school. He dropped out and joined the navy. When the war was over, Robert moved to Elyria, Ohio. He worked for Fruehauf, a trucking company. He married Marian, a West Virginia girl.

When it was time for Carl to go to high school, he walked five miles down a dirt road to Russellville, West Virginia, and caught the bus to Nuttall High School. The winters were bad, and there were many times he couldn't make it back up to his home. On those days, he stayed with the Haynes family in Russellville.

After graduating from Nuttall High School in 1948, Carl wanted to go to college. He picked wild blackberries and sold them for 50¢ a gallon. He earned enough to enroll in Beckley College in Beckley, West Virginia. That fall, he didn't have a car, but walking was not new to him. He rented a room from a family that lived on the hill behind what is now an Ollie's discount store. He got a job at a gas station at the comer of Johnstown Road and Kanawha Street.

Near the end of his first semester at Beckley College, Carl was told the gas station he worked at was going to close. They were going to widen Kanawha Street. Without a job, he had no choice but to return home. His mother, Lena, was a strong-willed woman. There were times Carl and his mother did not get along. After one argument, Carl packed his bags and hitchhiked to Roanoke, Virginia. He got a room at the YMCA where he paid for one night at a time. He found odd jobs—delivering flowers, washing dishes, etc. After a few weeks, he got sick. He bought a ticket for an all-night theater. He could get a drink of water, use the bathroom, and sleep. After a couple of days, he knew things had to change. He found the navy recruiter in Roanoke and tried to enlist in the navy. They asked if he had a high school diploma.

He answered, "Yes, but not with me."

They advised him he would get a better deal if he could produce his diploma. Carl hitchhiked back to Hickory Flats and asked his mother where his diploma was.

She replied, "In the dresser upstairs."

Carl went upstairs, got his diploma, and left the house. He later regretted. He did not stay long enough to see his father.

Carl hitchhiked to the navy recruiting office in Charleston, West Virginia, and enlisted. He was sent to Great Lakes, Illinois, for his boot camp training. He signed up for savings bonds and had them sent to his home in Hickory Flats after boot camp. He went to the aviation electronics school in Millington, Tennessee, just north of Memphis. He was there for a year and then had orders to Moffett Field near Sunnyvale, California. His brother Ray was in Oakland, California. He sent for his savings bonds and bought a car. Now he could visit his brother Ray.

My name is Loretta Faye Thurmon. I was born in the Santa Clara County Hospital in San Jose, California, October 11, 1932. I was raised in Campbell, California, just south of San Jose. My parents were Eldridge Luther Thurmon and Zona Bell Harness. My story is just the opposite from Carl's. I was first born. My only brother, Kenneth Royce, was born in January 1942. Carl lived in one house. We moved all over Campbell. I can remember five or six houses I lived in as a child. Carl had people around him, and they were all kin. I was surrounded by hundreds but kin to very few. Carl had to walk a mile to attend his one-room school. I walked four blocks to attend kindergarten. He walked on muddy roads. I walked on paved sidewalks. Where he had to go up and down hills, I walked on flat ground. Where he had bad winters, I had beautiful weather. I wore the same clothes all year. We had a rainy season in January, so I would wear a jacket. The Santa Clara Valley, where I was born, was known as the

Valley of Heart's Delight. Now this area is known as Silicon Valley. Carl had to walk five miles to catch a bus to go to high school. When I graduated from grammar school, I crossed the street to attend high school. Where Carl lived in West Virginia, the men had few choices. They could farm, work in the coal mines, or work in the timber. In Campbell, also known as Orchard City, we were surrounded by fruit trees, apricot, cherry, peach, pear, and prune. There were three canneries in the little town of Campbell and many more canneries in San Jose. People came from the Midwest, Arkansas, Oklahoma, Texas, etc. to work in the orchards and fruit canneries.

My great-grandfather Henry Fenwick left Bernie, Missouri, and moved to Orange County, California, in 1920. He wrote and encouraged his son-in-law, my grandfather Henry Thurmon, to join him. My grandmother Elizabeth Fenwick Thurmon died in childbirth in May 1911 when my father was two years old and my uncle Matthew was one year old. Bessie Caples was a fourteen-year-old orphaned girl who lived next door to Grandmother Elizabeth and was hired to help Grandmother. After Elizabeth's death, Grandfather Henry married Bessie Caples. She loved those boys and raised them as if they were her own. In 1925, my grandfather Henry; Grandma

Bessie; my dad, Eldridge; and my uncle Mack left Bernie, Missouri, and headed for California. They first joined the Fenwicks near Porterville, California, and worked in the orange groves. After they saw California, they never returned to Missouri.

My grandfather Marion Harrison Harness also had family that had moved to Porterville, California. They wanted him to join them. He owned a farm in Van Buren County, Arkansas. But it was the Depression; so in January 1931, he moved his family, which consisted of my grandmother Mary Louise and the Harness children—Bazzie, Auzzie, Zona, Thelda, and Kenneth—to Porterville where they worked in the orange groves. This was where my mother met my father.

When the work in the orange groves was completed, the Harness family and the Thurmon family relocated to the Campbell area at the end of the cannery season. The Harness family was returning to their farm in Van Buren County, Arkansas. My mother didn't want to go. She married my father on September 4, 1931, and stayed in California with the promise she would see her family every year if they didn't come to California. She would visit them in Arkansas. The next spring, the Harness family returned to Campbell to work in the fruit. This continued for many years.

In 1934, my grandfather Henry Thurmon passed away. Grandma Bessie moved in with us.

In 1936, the Harness family returned to Campbell to work. My aunt Thelda met and married Ray Gammon when her family returned to Arkansas that fall. She remained in Campbell. My father bought a house at 22 Dillion Avenue. Grandma Bessie bought a house trailer and put it in our backyard.

September of 1938, I started first grade. In late November, I came down with scarlet fever. I was taken to Santa Clara County Hospital and put in quarantine. The school was closed. No other child came down with it. Before Christmas, my mother came to the hospital thinking she was taking me home. Now the doctors told her I had measles and had to stay at the hospital. A few weeks later, she returned to the hospital again thinking she was taking me home. Now the doctors told her I needed a double mastoid operation. After my operation, I was left with the hearing loss of 50 percent in my right ear and 75 percent in my left ear. I had been in the hospital so long and missed so much school I had to repeat the first grade. In 1939, my father sold the house on Dillon Avenue; and we moved to Sunnyvale, California, where my father started a taxicab company. Earlier, Mom, Dad, and I traveled to Arkansas. I was left with my grandmother Mary Harness while my parents traveled on to Detroit, Michigan, and my father picked up two brand-new Hudsons. He painted them maroon and cream. These were his taxicabs. His friend Lloyd Loveday was his partner. The phone number on the side of the taxicab was for a bar. They would take turns sitting at the bar waiting for a call. After a year, my father sold his half of the cab company to his friend Lloyd Loveday. We moved back to Campbell, and my dad bought a house on Casey Road. He was also buying the Richfield gas station at the corner of Winchester Road and Campbell Avenue across from the grammar school.

Things were good. I had Grandma Bessie. I had Aunt Thelda and Uncle Ray and my uncle Mac. Uncle Mac had married Eunice Stapp; and they had a baby girl, Maxine, born in November 1936.

In December 7, 1941, we were at war. My father had let men charge gasoline, and now they joined the military and left owing my dad money. My uncle Ray and my uncle Mac joined the army. At our house on Casey Road, we had a large yard, a Victory garden. We also had a cow, chickens, and rabbits.

My grandma Bessie bought a three-room house on Gilman Avenue, just down the street from my aunt Thelda. My aunt Thelda, Grandma Bessie, and my mom all worked at the Hunt's fruit cannery down the street. My dad struggled but ended up losing the gas station. My brother, Kenneth Royce, was born on January 25, 1942.

The war was now over. Things had changed. Uncle Mac, divorced from Eunice, was now married to Lena Bowles; and they had Elizabeth. Aunt Thelda, now divorced from Uncle Ray Gammon, was living with Jack Silverbar; and they had Brenda.

My dad wanted to change. He found a listing for a gas station / motel not far from my mother's family in Arkansas. He sold the house on Casey Road, sold all of the furniture, and put our few belongings in the back of a pickup truck. I rode with my dad. My mother drove another car with Royce, Aunt Thelda, and Brenda. Aunt Thelda was returning to her family in Arkansas a few days into our trip. My aunt Thelda gave my mother a ring to be given to me when I was old enough to take care of it. It had a quarter-carat diamond in an old-fashioned setting. My mother put it on the ring finger of her right hand.

We arrived in Arkansas. My dad went and looked at the gas station / motel. It was a dump. We stayed with my grandparents that winter. I attended school in Clinton, Arkansas. By spring, my dad had all the bad weather he could take, so we headed back to Campbell, California. We stayed with Grandma Bessie. My dad bought a lot near the corner of Winchester Road and Rosemary Lane and had a new home built. He also rented a lot on the corner of Gilman Avenue and Campbell Avenue and started a used-car lot because the schools in Arkansas were far behind the California schools. I was kept back another year.

My dad did well in the used-car business. It wasn't long before he purchased a nice big lot on Winchester Road across from the A&W Root Beer stand. My mother had gone back to work at the cannery and was now a forelady at Hunt's in Campbell.

In the summertime when I was thirteen and fourteen years old, I would pack a lunch for my brother, and we would walk next door to the apricot orchard. It was owned by the Lamorte family. I would cut apricots for 10¢ a box. This would help pay for my school clothes. Later in the summer, I would walk to the other end of the orchard and pick prunes for the Lamorte family. I would also get 10¢ a box for the prunes. Many years later, the orchards would be gone, and a strip mall and apartment complex would take their place. The dirt roads that I learned to drive a car on are now called Cadillac Drive and Impala Drive.

In early June 1948, I started working at the Hunt's fruit cannery. I was only fifteen years old at the time, but I lied about my age. I would not be sixteen until October. My dad would take half of my paychecks to pay for my room and board.

I started out on a grape shaker. I was paid $1 an hour. I thought I was making good money. Grandma Bessie and my mother worked in the same cannery, but I only saw them at lunchtime. I worked in the pears, and Grandma Bessie worked in the peaches. When school started that fall, I quit the cannery and went back to school.

The next year, 1949, when the cannery started up, they put me on a pear machine. I made more money. It was piecework, and you were paid by how many pears you cut. My uncle Mac supplied my machine with fruit. He was so proud of me. I never missed a pear. He would read my machine at the end of the day and tell me I was cutting more pears than the older ladies.

When school started in September 1949, I quit the cannery and started my freshman year at high school. I liked school but never got to attend any school functions. I was the babysitter and had to get home to care for my brother who got out of school one-half hour before I did. We walked a quarter mile down Winchester Road, along a peach orchard, to get to our house. I always got home first. He played along the way.

In January 1950, Grandma Bessie sold her house on Gilman Avenue and bought a trailer that was in a trailer park on Dillon Avenue.

In April, my mother said she was leaving my father this time for good. She was getting a divorce. She was driving back to Arkansas with my brother and I to live with her family. I missed the last six weeks of my freshman year at high school and missed all of my final tests. About eight weeks later, my father showed up in Arkansas. Not sure what he promised her, but we ended up going back to Campbell just in time for the cannery season to start. I was back at my pear machine. When school started in September, I went in and officially quit. The kids I started kindergarten with would now be seniors. I would be a freshman. I returned to the cannery and worked to the end of the season. When the fruit season was done in Campbell, I moved into the house trailer with Grandma Bessie. We worked in the tomatoes for a Hunt's cannery in San Jose. A couple living in the trailer across from hers also worked there and gave us a ride. That was where I was working when I turned eighteen.

My parents liked to go out and play cards with their friends. As soon as the tomato season was over, they wanted me home to babysit my brother.

Early the next spring, I stayed with Grandma Bessie again. Now we were packing cherries in San Jose, and again we rode with the couple in the trailer park. When the cherries were done, I moved back home.

One day in early May, while walking down Campbell Avenue, I ran into a boy I knew from high school. His name was Bill High. While he was in school, he worked for my dad at the used-car lot, washing cars and doing odd jobs. After graduation, he joined the navy. While he was away at boot camp, his best friend married his girlfriend, and now he was home on a thirty-day leave and had nowhere to go. He offered me a ride home. Every few days, he would show up, and we would go out and get a hamburger. On the last day of his leave, he told me he had been invited to a party and wanted me to go with him. I knew everyone that would be there. They lived on Dillon and Gilman avenues.

The Korean War had broken out, and the Kennedy brothers had joined the army. Their girlfriends, Ella Holland and Pat Jones, were having a going-away party for them on Friday night. On the way to the party, Bill stopped the car and pulled out an engagement ring. I was surprised and didn't want to take it. I looked at Bill as a friend, not a boyfriend. Bill said the people at the party were expecting me to be wearing the ring. I felt trapped. I put the ring on.

After the party, Bill took me home. As we stood on my front porch, I gave the ring back to Bill. He was leaving early the next morning on a bus heading for San Diego. I told him I would write to him. I did not know that Bill had dropped the ring into my coat pocket. I went inside the house and laid my coat on a chair by the door. Many times when I went somewhere, I would bring my little brother a candy bar, pack of gum, etc.

The next morning, after the party, I slept in. My little brother went through my coat pocket and found the ring. He showed it to my mother.

She told him, "She probably got it from a box of Cracker Jacks."

Later when I woke up, my brother mentioned the ring. He said he would rather have gum. I explained to him that it didn't come out of a box of Cracker Jacks and I needed to have it back.

A few days later, Pat and Ella called and invited me to go with them to Bert's country inn. I had never been there. It was what they called a roadhouse or honkytonk. It sat back in a prune orchard at the end of Campbell Avenue. A family from Campbell had a family band and would be playing there that night. I went with them.

God works in mysterious ways!

When you left the main gate at Moffett Field Naval Air Station and crossed over Bayshore Highway, you would be on Sunnyvale Road. A few miles down this road, you would come to the intersection of Sunnyvale Road and Campbell Avenue. Bert's country inn sat back in a prune orchard.

Carl and his friends had been there a few times. When Ella and Pat and I went in, there was a couch along the wall. We sat down. There were a lot of young people there. I enjoyed the music. Sam High came over and talked to me. He was Bill's cousin and also worked for my dad. I noticed three sailors sitting at a table. They were in their navy uniforms. One of them kept looking at me. It made me very uncomfortable. After a while, he came over and asked me to dance. The band was playing "Tennessee Waltz." I told him I didn't know how to dance, which was true, but we tried. He didn't know how to dance either.

He took hold of my right wrist and led me to the table where his friends were sitting. I didn't feel threatened. I was surrounded by people I knew. He said his name was Carl Amick, and he asked my name. I said it was Hazel. He introduced me to his friends Karl Brashera and Willis Alston. They were drinking beer and offered to buy me one.

I said, "No, thank you. I don't drink."

Willis Alston offered me a cigarette.

I said, "Thank you, but I don't smoke."

Willis remarked, "A California girl that doesn't drink or smoke? That's unusual."

Carl commented on how pretty my ring was (until I could get the ring back to Bill, I wore it so I would know where it was; my little brother, Royce, was always in my things). After a couple of hours of listening to the music and watching people dance, the girls wanted to leave. So did I. Carl offered to take me home.

But I said, "No, thank you. I would go with the girls."

A few days later, the phone rang. I answered.

A voice said, "Is Hazel there?"

I had forgotten about the sailor and said no.

Then he asked, "Is Loretta there?"

I said, "Yes, this is Loretta. Who is this?"

He replied, "This is the sailor you met the other night at Bert's."

I said, "How did you get this number?"

He said he talked to Sam High and Sam gave him one of my dad's business cards with our home phone number on it. Sam told him my name was Loretta. Carl said he wanted to take me out on Wednesday night and would pick me up at 6:00 p.m. Our home address was also on the card Sam gave him.

I called Pat and said, "You got me into this. You'll have to get me out of it."

They were going to pick me up at 5:30 p.m., and we would go to the local park. On Wednesday evening, Grandma Bessie was at our house along with my parents and friends Wendell and Mary Pounds. At 5:30 p.m., I was in the kitchen dressed in blue jeans and a shirt with my foot propped up on the table, and I was painting my toenails.

I heard someone say, "She's in the kitchen."

I thought it was the girls. When I looked up, Carl was standing in the doorway.

He said, "I'm not taking you out dress like that. Go put on a dress."

I got up and went into the bedroom.

Grandma Bessie followed me in there and said, "This is the one you will marry. When he says frog, you jump."

Carl must've thought we were rich. My father's new Packard and Wendell's new Cadillac were parked in our driveway.

Carl had on gray slacks, shirt, tie, and a gray jacket. He never wore his uniform on a date. He took me to a nice restaurant on Bayshore Drive, Dinah's Shack. I didn't talk much. I was afraid I would say the wrong thing.

When he took me home later, he said, "I finally found a girl who keeps her mouth shut."

I didn't know if that was a good thing or a bad thing.

A few days later, Carl called and asked to take me out again. I enjoyed myself the first time, and I said okay. During the week, I had received a picture of Bill High that he sent from San Diego. I set it on the mantle. When Carl arrived at our house, I wasn't quite ready. Grandma Bessie opened the door and let Carl in. He saw the picture on the mantle and asked if that was Bill. Grandma Bessie said yes. Carl walked over and turned Bill's picture to the wall. She had to come in my bedroom and tell me about it.

On this date, Carl took me to another nice restaurant called Rick's Place. I enjoyed the meal and told him, although I enjoyed it, I would be just as happy with a hamburger at a drive-in. I also told him that I had a hearing problem and that was why I was so quiet. After that, he made sure I was looking at him when he was talking to me.

My mother decided it was time for her Arkansas trip before the cannery season started. She wanted my brother and I to go with her. I loved my Arkansas family and always looked forward to our yearly visit. The next time Carl called, I explained I was going to Arkansas with my mother and would be gone for two weeks.

While I was in Arkansas, Carl was driving in San Jose and went to a flashing yellow light. Someone went through a flashing red light and T-boned him. His car was totaled. Back then, you didn't have to have insurance.

We came back from Arkansas. Grandma Bessie told me Carl had been calling asking if we were back yet. Later Carl called and said he had tickets to the Ice Capades at the Cow Palace in San Francisco. His friend Richard was going to drive us and asked if I could find a blind date for Richard. I ran next door and asked Babe Galliasso if she would like to go to the Ice Capades. She said yes.

This was our third date. Richard and Babe were in the front seat. Carl and I were in the backseat. I noticed his tie was crooked. I reached over and straightened it.

He smiled and said, "You would be handy to have around. Marry me."

I said, "No!"

He said, "Why not?"

I said, "Because you're joking."

We enjoyed the Ice Capades. The next few times Carl came over, I noticed he was in a different car. He finally told me how his car got wrecked. He was borrowing cars from his friends on the base after we were married. He confessed he had even rented a couple of cars.

In 1951, the cannery season started. I was back at my pear machine. My mother was driving a 1939 Plymouth coupe to work every day. My dad had used whitewash, and there was a price on the windshield, $99.99. I bought the car. My dad said I wasn't old enough to have the car put in my name, so he was going to register it in his name.

I said, "If I can't have it in my name, put it in Carl's name."

My dad said, "If you do that, Carl can just walk away with that car."

I replied, "I would rather have him cheat me out of it than you!"

I had written to Bill and told him I needed to get the ring back to him. One Saturday morning, Bill called. He had taken emergency leave and came back to Campbell. He wanted to talk. I told him to come to my house. Before Bill got there, Carl arrived. I didn't expect Carl. I thought he had the duty. I asked Carl to go in the kitchen with my mother and let me talk to Bill.

Carl said, "No! I'm sitting on the couch."

Bill was on one side; Carl on the other. Bill knew I was surprised when he gave me the ring; so finally he got up, took the ring and his picture, and left. Bill would make someone a good husband but not me.

Not long after the cannery season started, Grandma Bessie suffered a stroke. She was paralyzed on one side. After a stay in the hospital, she was taken to a nursing home in Los Gatos, not far from Campbell.

Carl had duty every fourth night. On many nights when he could leave the base, he would hitch-hike to our house. When I came home from work, he would be waiting. He told me that, in boot camp, the sailors were told not to get married until they made first class because they couldn't afford it. Carl said he would make first class in September. He wanted to get married. He asked my mother to get him a job at the cannery starting September 1. He would take a month's leave and stay at our house, and by the end of September, he would have made enough money for us to get married. When Carl stayed at our house, he slept in my bed in a room I shared with my brother. I got the couch.

Carl stayed at our house on the night of August 31. I drove him to Moffett Field on September 1 to pick up his leave papers and his clothes. After a few minutes, he came out and told me there was a telegram waiting for him at the base. His grandfather Lee Amick had passed away. The telegram said they were waiting for him. He got a flight out of Moffett Field to Maryland. From there, he hitchhiked back to Hickory Flats. As he got near the house, he saw them coming home from the cemetery. They had not waited for him. The next day, Carl called to say he was spending September in West Virginia. He wanted to spend time with his dad and do some hunting.

Carl had taken my picture with him to West Virginia and put it on the mantle. He told his mother that, if he had not come to West Virginia, he would have gotten married at the end of September. She was not happy. His brother Fred married a California girl. His brother Ray married a California girl. She did not want Carl to marry a California girl.

The next Sunday, Carl took his mother to church at Sugar Grove. A girl Carl had gone to school with was in the congregation. Carl's mother invited the girl to come home and have dinner with them. She accepted. The next Sunday at church, Carl's mother invited her to dinner again and again. She accepted. Carl's mother suggested he take the girl to the homecoming football game at their old high school. The girl wanted to go. Carl would never hurt anyone's feelings, so they went.

Carl felt bad that he couldn't afford to get me a ring.

I told him, "I have a ring. My mother is wearing it."

I told my mother I wanted the ring that Aunt Thelda gave me. She didn't want to give it up and told me she couldn't get it off of her finger. I rubbed her hand with Crisco. I almost broke her finger, but I got the ring off. While Carl was in West Virginia, I took the ring to a local jeweler. The jeweler put my diamond in a used setting that came with a wedding band.

At the end of September, Carl returned from West Virginia. I showed him the ring. He liked it, but he had a guilty conscience about seeing the other girl. He told me about it.

I was upset and told him, "There is the door. Goodbye. Don't come back."

He kept coming back. We would go get a hamburger, but no more was said about getting married.

On Halloween, we were invited to my friend Pat's house for a party. I never wore the ring. He knew I kept it in the top drawer of my dresser. On the way to Pat's house, Carl stopped the car, took the ring out of his pocket, and asked me to marry him. I said yes.

Later he would say, "I should have known I was marrying a witch. I got engaged on Halloween."

The cannery season was over in late September. I babysat for two different neighbors. On Friday, the day after Thanksgiving, I had been gone most of the afternoon babysitting. I was surprised to see Carl sitting on the couch talking to my mother. He had hitchhiked from the base. Although the car was in his name, he didn't have the special sticker to get it on the base.

My mother said, "Carl has bad news," then she got up and went in the kitchen.

I asked Carl about the bad news.

Carl said he had orders to report to San Diego on January 1, 1952, and then he said, "I'm taking you with me."

I said okay.

Carl said that he already had his blood work done at Moffett Field. On the next day, Saturday, we went to San Jose and got my blood work done. When the tests were done, they were to be sent to Dr. Wade in Campbell to be signed. Next we went to the jewelry store to get Carl's wedding ring. We had it engraved with our initials, but no date just in case something went wrong. Next stop was a florist. Carl ordered an orchid corsage to be picked up the following Saturday morning.

We had been attending St. Paul's Methodist Church in San Jose. We went there the next day, Sunday, and put a note in the collection plate. We needed to talk to the minister. After church, we went in his study, and Carl told him we wanted to get married. The following Saturday, December 1, 1951, he counseled us and then agreed to marry us. Carl explained it would be a very small wedding, no family. The minister said that he would supply a maid of honor and a best man. On Monday morning, I drove Carl back to Moffett Field.

Since Grandma Bessie had her stroke, her trailer had been sitting empty. The normal fee was $15 a month, but the Lydell family who owned the trailer park were friends of my dad's and didn't charge him anything for it to sit there empty. On Monday morning, I went to the nursing home to tell Grandma Bessie that Carl and I were getting married and wanted to stay in her trailer. She couldn't talk, but she nodded her head. Later I went and talked to Mrs. Lydell and told her I was getting married on December 1 and would be living in the trailer for a month and gave her $15. Then I went to the trailer, changed the bedding, and gave it a good cleaning.

When I had my blood work done at the lab in San Jose, I was told it should be in Campbell at Dr. Wade's office by Tuesday. Tuesday afternoon, I called Dr. Wade. He said nothing had arrived from San Jose. I called again on Wednesday. Again, nothing. I called the lab in San Jose on Thursday. They said the postage had come off of the envelope and it had been returned to their office. There wasn't time to remail it. I would have to go to San Jose and pick it up.

My mother had taken my car that morning, which wasn't unusual. She got back home at two o'clock to pick up something and was going back out. I told her I needed my car and I had to go to San Jose. She questioned me on why I needed to go to San Jose. I finally told her I was getting married on Saturday and had to go to the lab and pick up results from my blood work.

My dad was standing there and said, "That's just like you. Once you're old enough to pay me back for raising you, you get married."

My reply was "I didn't ask to be born."

I got in my car and drove to San Jose, picked up the paperwork, drove straight to Dr. Wade's office, and had him sign it. On Friday, I went grocery shopping and took groceries to the trailer. Carl had duty Friday night.

It had rained a lot in November. Creeks were flooding. It rained all night. I left home at eight o'clock on the morning of December 1 to go pick Carl up at Moffett Field. When I got near the base, the right-hand side of Bayshore Highway was blocked off because of high water. Back then, Bayshore Highway was just two lanes. A policeman was stopping traffic and turning some people back.

When I approached the policeman, I started crying and told him, "This is my wedding day. I am getting married at 1:00 p.m., and my boyfriend is at Moffett Field."

He let me pass.

Once Carl got in the car, we headed for the courthouse in San Jose to pick up our marriage license. There were two other couples ahead of us. When it was our turn, it didn't take long. They looked at our paperwork, asked a few questions, and issued us a license.

Next we went to the jewelry store and picked up Carl's ring, on to the florist to get my orchid corsage, then back to my parents' house to get ready. I didn't have time to buy anything new. I got married in a gray suit that I wore to church. Carl wore the gray slacks and gray jacket that he wore on our first date. My mother, my father, and my little brother attended our wedding.

St. Paul's Methodist Church was in a busy part of town, right behind a Hale's department store. They had put barricades up to reserve parking for us. Carl parked our '39 Plymouth, and my parents pulled in behind us in a brand-new Packard.

I was surprised to see quite a few people there.

The minister had announced to the congregation, "This young couple are getting married, and they are welcome to attend."

Another surprise, Mrs. Smith, my music teacher from high school, sang at our wedding. The minister's wife made us a three-layer wedding cake with white icing and a perfect white rose on the top as a decoration. We thought it was a beautiful wedding.

As we were leaving the church and getting into our cars, my mother said, "You both look so nice all dressed up. Why don't you drive the Packard home, and we will take your Plymouth."

Carl said okay.

As were pulling away from the curb, my mother said, "Oh, by the way, it needs gas."

At this point, we were out of money. We spent $3 on the license, money for his ring, and money for my corsage; paid the minister $10; and gave Mrs. Smith $5 for singing. On the way home, we saw a gas station having its grand opening. If you bought gas, which was 10¢ a gallon, you would get a free hot dog. This was our wedding dinner.

After eating our hot dogs and getting a few gallons of gas, we arrived back at my parents' home, where I got my few remaining things. As I've mentioned before, I was the babysitter a lot of dates. Carl and I went on. I had to take my brother, Royce, with me. On this day, as we were getting into the Plymouth, Royce started to crawl in.

Carl got him by the shoulder and said, "No MORE."

Carl had never been to Grandma Bessie's trailer. It was on the opposite side of town from our home on Winchester Road. He had no idea what to expect. He carried me over the threshold. As you stepped into the door, there was a bed on the right, a small refrigerator on the left, and a small chest of drawers next to the head of the bed with a lamp. The kitchen had a sink and an apartment-sized gas stove with an oven. The oven was our only source of heat. The kitchen table was across from the stove. It was all we needed.

Grandma Bessie had two iron skillets, a large one and a small one; a saucepan; a percolator to make coffee; a spatula; and some assorted plates and silverware. I didn't have a wedding shower, so we were thankful for these things. There were two trailers between us and the washhouse. The washhouse was a cinderblock building with toilets and showers. The men went in the right side of the building, and the women went in the left.

The navy paid the sailors on the first and fifteenth of the month. If those dates fell on the weekend, you would wait until the next business day to get your check. Later this would be changed, and payday would be every other Friday. Since we had no money and Carl wouldn't get paid until Monday, the groceries I had put in the trailer on Friday came in handy. On Monday morning, as Carl went to the washhouse for his shower, I cooked a nice breakfast—bacon, eggs, hash brown potatoes, and coffee. After we ate, I drove him to Moffett Field. At four o'clock in the evening, I would go back to Moffett Field and pick him up. This was our routine for the next four weeks.

On December 28, Carl packed his uniforms in the '39 Plymouth and headed for San Diego. He had to report to the Thirty-Second Street Naval Station on January 1, 1952. He didn't want me in the trailer by myself, and he didn't know how long it would be before he found us an apartment in San Diego. My father wanted to gut the trailer, move it to his car lot, and use it to store his tools where he could lock them up. So I took the bedding, towels, dishes, and kitchen utensils and moved back to my parents' home.

Carl called me every night. Ten days later, when he called, he had found us an apartment at 166 Sixteenth Street in San Diego. The next morning, I took two cardboard boxes to the train station in Campbell to be shipped to San Diego.

When I went to buy my ticket, the ticket master, a friend of my father, said, "If she was my daughter, I wouldn't let her get on that train. The tracks below Santa Barbara are underwater. Not sure when the train will get through."

I returned to my parents' home. Around midnight, the phone rang. It was Carl.

He said, "The boxes arrived. Where are you?" He had taken the boxes to our apartment.

I explained to him what happened.

He said, "Get on an airplane and fly to San Diego."

I arrived at Lindbergh Field in San Diego at 9:00 a.m. the next day. At that time, the Lindbergh Field terminal was about the size of the bottom floor of the house I live in now. Carl had no problem finding me.

The furnished apartment at 166 Sixteenth Street was on the third floor of an old hotel. The rent was $60 a month. The city buses parked in behind, and when they started the buses up at 6:00 a.m. every day, that was Carl's alarm clock. I fixed our breakfast every morning, then Carl would drive to the base.

Because I had packed cherries, worked in the pears, and worked in the tomatoes the year before, I could draw unemployment. Every Wednesday, I would walk four blocks over to B Street, turn left, and walk sixteen blocks down to the waterfront and the unemployment office and collect $15. We found Tops Drive Inn, where we could get a cup of hot chocolate loaded with whipped cream for 50¢. We also found a Chinese American restaurant where a breaded veal cutlet, salad, vegetable, dessert, and drink was 85¢. We would go there once a month as a treat. After a couple of months, we knew we were expecting Steven. We saw an ad in the paper from a furniture store. They had baby cribs on sale for $39. This was our first piece of furniture.

I fell in love with San Diego, and I loved walking down to the waterfront. Time flew by. Now it was Fourth of July weekend. Carl's squadron, the 702/145, was preparing to go aboard the USS *Kearsarge*, an aircraft carrier. This was the last weekend Carl would be allowed to leave the San Diego area and take me back home. We packed our belongings and Steven's crib into the trunk of the '39 Plymouth and headed for Campbell. Carl flew back to San Diego. His squadron went aboard the USS *Kearsarge* and headed for Japan on their way to Korea.

USS Kearsarge (CV-33)

My allotment check was $127 a month. My father took half of that for my room and board. Carl's brother Ray and his wife, Georgia, came down from Oakland to see me a couple of times. The first few weeks, I drove to the clinic at Moffett Field for my checkups. The last two weeks, I had to go to Oak Knoll Naval Hospital in Oakland for my checkups. This worked. On Wednesdays, my father went to the auto auction in Oakland. He would drop me off at the hospital at 8:00 a.m. and pick me up when the auction was over.

Early on the morning of September 11, 1952, my parents drove me to Oak Knoll Naval Hospital and then went home. Steven was born later that day. The Red Cross sent Carl a telegram. Ray and Georgia felt bad they were out of town visiting her parents. My mother came back three days later and took Steven and I back to Campbell. When Steven was a few weeks old, I took him to the nursing home so Grandma Bessie could see him. Her eyes lit up, and she smiled.

On April 25, 1953, I took the train to San Diego and spent the night at the Horton Hotel; and the next morning, I took the ferry across the bay and watched the USS *Kearsarge* pull into the harbor. I had not seen Carl for nine and a half months. I thought we would take the train back to Campbell, but he wanted to fly. He was so anxious to see Steven.

The squadron 702/145 would now be stationed at Naval Air Station Miramar, just north of San Diego. We already had an apartment at 101 Torrey Pines, Military Housing, and now with Steven's things, there was no way everything we had would fit in the back of the '39 Plymouth. I had purchased a one-wheel trailer from my dad for $10. We loaded up the trailer and headed for our apartment—it was partially furnished. It had twin beds and a dresser in the bedroom, a kitchen table and three chairs, and an apartment-sized gas stove. We needed to buy a refrigerator and a washing machine. A few days later, our neighbor was moving. We bought their couch for $5. We took one of the twin beds out of the bedroom to make room for Steven's crib. A few weeks later, we bought a seventeen-inch table-model TV and a double bed. We were high on a plateau looking down on the Pacific Ocean. Carl made antenna out of an aluminum tubing and a beer can. It worked great. We could get San Diego and Los Angeles.

One day, Carl came home from work driving a 1942 Chevrolet coupe. He had traded cars with somebody on the base. When the weather was nice, which was most of the time, I would have a dinner that we could take to the beach and eat. Steven loved the water. We only had to drive about a quarter of a mile, then walked down the cliff on a path, and we would be on the beach.

Torrey Pines, at one time, was the housing for an army base during World War II. The base had been torn down. Only the paved roads remained. The portion that had been the base is now known as Torrey Pines Golf Course where they hold the Andy Williams Open every year. The housing area where we lived is now the Jonas Salk Institute.

In September 1953, Carl wanted to take thirty days' leave and go to West Virginia. He wanted his father to meet Steven. We arrived in West Virginia. Carl's mother told me how she did not want Carl to marry a California girl and had invited this other girl over. Then I knew Carl was telling me the truth. Steven celebrated his first birthday in West Virginia, and now we were expecting baby number two.

That Christmas, my dad bought Steven a rocking horse. It was red and made out of wood. Steven named it Nong Nong. That was what he would say when he rode it.

Right after Christmas 1953, the 702/145 was told they were going aboard the USS *Randolph*, another aircraft carrier, for a goodwill tour of the Mediterranean. They would be gone for eight months, which meant I would have another baby by myself.

USS Randolph (*CV-15*)

The USS *Randolph* went to sea now that I was expecting a second child. I could apply for a two-bedroom apartment. My new apartment was at 204 Torrey Pines. My friend Mary lived behind me. She was also expecting her second child, so they were moving into a two-bedroom also. I paid for the truck, and Mary's husband and his friend did all my heavy lifting. The small stuff I put in boxes and carried into my apartment by myself. I was wearing Carl's shirt. After I got settled in, I showered and put on my maternity smock. I was sitting in my front yard. Steven was riding Nong Nong. The sailor that lived across the way came over to apologize. He watched me carry the boxes and didn't realize I was pregnant. He thought I was just fat. He was being transferred and wanted me to have the little white picket fence he had built for his own yard. He came over and installed it.

A few days later, I was sitting in the yard reading. Steven was riding Nong Nong. A little boy older than Steven came riding by on his tricycle. He got off, walked into our yard, and walked over to Nong Nong. Steven got off and let him ride. After a little while, Steven walked over to the tricycle. The little boy ran over and pushed Steven down. I led the little boy out of our yard and shut the gate. I put Steven in the car, and we drove to Sears. I went into the toy department and found a beautiful little green tricycle. It was the nicest one they had. It was $25. It was a little big for him, but I figured he would grow into it. I opened up a charge account and would pay $5 a month. When I got the tricycle back to our apartment, Steven couldn't reach the pedals. The nice sailor across the way had some wood and put blocks on the pedals. Now Steven could reach them. He loved his tricycle as much as he loved Nong Nong.

My due date for Richard was the second week of May. That date came and went. I gained fifty pounds with Steven. The doctor didn't want me to do that again. I was on a strict diet. I only gained twenty pounds with Richard. The third week of May, I got the flu. My mother called to check on me, and when she heard I was sick, she got on the bus and came to La Jolla. I got a letter from Carl telling me to send another telegram. He had not gotten the first one. I was taking hot baths. I was jumping off chairs. I was hitting the speed bumps at the abandoned old army camp. Nothing worked. Richard would arrive when Richard was ready.

I went into labor about midnight. Richard was born on June 5, 1954. I had some problems. I had already gotten a letter from Carl to tell the Red Cross to get him home. A Red Cross representative came into my room, and I explained my situation. They flew Carl home. It took five days. I picked Carl up at the airport and dropped my mother off at the bus station. That evening, my neighbor across the way was having a Guardian Service dinner. She was short a couple and asked if Carl and I could come. The dinner was good. After we ate, I went back to our apartment, where the babies were sleeping. Later, when Carl came home, he told me he bought the whole set of Guardian cookware. Now we could retire Grandma Bessie's things. A few weeks after Carl returned, we went to the Chevrolet dealer in La Jolla and traded our 1942 Chevy coupe and on a 1952 Chevy coupe.

In August, his squadron, the 702/145, returned to Naval Air Station Miramar.

I had not been feeling good. I thought I was just tired now with two babies to take care of. Carl suggested I go to the base and get a good checkup. They did some tests and told me to come back in a week. I returned to the clinic the next week and was told I was pregnant. I went home and started dinner. Carl came home later and said, in a few months, the 702/145 would be going aboard the USS *Boxer*. I sat down on the floor and started crying. I told him I was pregnant and I could not have another baby by myself. He said he had been wanting to go to B-school in Millington and this would be a good time to apply for it.

Carl received orders to Aviation Electronic B-School in Millington, Tennessee. Millington is just north of Memphis. This time, we would need a moving van. We placed our luggage on the floor of the back seat and placed a piece of heavy cardboard over that to make a flat surface for the babies. We put blankets and pillows back there to make them comfortable. The box with Grandma Bessie's pots and pans went in the trunk, along with extra blankets. It would be wintertime in Tennessee. When we got to Memphis, our car had a problem. We found a motel with a kitchenette next to a gas station. They let Carl work on our car. I had grandma's box so I could fix meals. In a few days, the car was repaired. Now we needed to find a place to live.

Carl found a listing for a furnished attic apartment on Autumn Street in Memphis. They only wanted short-term renters because the house was up for sale. Our furniture went into storage, and Carl checked in to the B-school. We were in the attic apartment about ten days, then Carl found a duplex on Atlantic Avenue. On the day our furniture was to arrive, Carl dropped me off at the duplex and went on to school. By the time he came back at 4:00 p.m., what few things we had were in place. Steven was happy to see Nong Nong and his tricycle. We went to a secondhand furniture store and purchased a chest of drawers for our bedroom, bunk beds and a chest of drawers for the boys, a kitchen table and four chairs, and a green sectional couch. Later we would get a wooden chest for a toy box.

After a couple of weeks, Carl started tutoring a couple of men who were attending B-school. I always had dinner on the table when Carl came in. As soon as we ate, the table would be cleared, and men would arrive. One night, Carl brought company home for dinner. It was Willis Alston. I had not seen Willis since the night I met Carl. Willis was attending B-school and needed tutoring. Willis was from Kilgore, Texas. His older sister was Alice Lon. At that time, Alice Lon was Lawrence Welk's Champagne Lady. Later, after Eugene was born, we would go to Kilgore, Texas, and attend Willis Alston's wedding.

At the end of every two weeks of school, there would be a test. If you passed the test, you went on to the next level. Carl would joke and tell me I had to have this baby on a Friday after his test. That way, he could take leave and not have to repeat any of the schooling. That's exactly what I did. Eugene was born on Saturday morning, June 4, 1955. They gave me a saddle block. I'd never had one before. I did not know I had to lie flat. When Carl came to see me and the baby, I asked for a pillow to put under my head. The nurse handed Carl one. I had terrible headaches. I was also upset because I spent Richard's first birthday in the hospital. I was on morphine for a few days. Carl took two weeks' leave.

Carl completed B-school in mid-December. Now he had orders for Hutchinson, Kansas, but wanted to spend Christmas in West Virginia. He wanted his dad to see his three sons. The moving van came; and our furniture was taken to Hutchinson, Kansas, and put in storage. In West Virginia, I met his brother Robert for the first time. He was taking pictures with the flash camera, and he would throw the used flashbulbs into the fireplace. Carl told him not to do that. After one flashbulb exploded, Steven put his hand to his eye. I looked at it. Everything looked fine. Later, when Steven started school, we found out he had 20/200 vision. I always felt it had something to do with that exploding flashbulb.

After Christmas, we headed for Hutchinson, Kansas. We found a motel with a kitchenette, got Grandma Bessie's box out of the trunk, and started looking for a place to live. After a week or so, we found a house for sale at Nineteenth Street and Halsey Drive. It had two bedrooms and one bath with a nice big yard.

Carl would be stationed at the Hutchinson Naval Air Station near Haven, Kansas. Haven was in Amish community. The boys loved to see the beautiful little horses pulling the carriages. We lived in that house a little over a year. One of Carl's jobs was to fly to Guantanamo Bay, Cuba. The windshields of the airplanes would be blacked out, and the pilots would have to find their way back to the runway using instruments. Carl was the radioman. On one of those trips, Carl came home to find me with an abscess tooth. There was no naval hospital in the area. I was admitted to St. Elizabeth Catholic Hospital and ran up a large bill. Carl had to take a month's leave. About the same time, Carl made chief petty officer. He would have to buy all new uniforms and would get reimbursed later.

Carl told me, before we were married, he never wanted me to work outside the home. He wanted me to be there when he came home from work at night, and we would live on what he made. But this was an emergency. We needed money for those uniforms and to pay off my hospital bill. Carl made arrangements to work three nights a week at the base and, during the day, to drive a taxicab. I got a job as a carhop and worked from 6:00 p.m. until midnight five days a week. It worked out that we only needed a babysitter for one night a week. I was paid $1 an hour but got a lot of money in tips since I would be at the car window. Looking at them, I could figure out what they ordered.

As soon as we had the money in the bank to pay for the uniforms and paid off my hospital bill, we both quit our second jobs.

We had picked up another tricycle, a little red one. This was Richard's. It was too cold to play outside, so the boys rode their tricycles in the house. One afternoon, Richard made a quick turn in the kitchen, turned his tricycle over, and hit his head on a gallon milk jug that was sitting on the bottom shelf. It peeled the back of his head. Carl was in a carpool. I had our car that day. I got the boys into their coats, wrapped a towel around Richard's head, and got the boys into the car. At the same moment, Carl pulled into the driveway. He jumped in our car, and we raced to the hospital. They didn't put stitches in the back of Richard's head. They put twelve clamps.

About the time we found out I was pregnant with Ronda, the base informed the men that Hutchinson Naval Air Station was closing and would be turned over to the Kansas National Guard and, if they owned a home, to sell it. I was reading the newspaper and saw an ad where someone wanted to sell a brand-new 1957 Buick station wagon. It had five miles on it. They would take a house or car in trade. Carl called the number in the paper. They took our house and the '52 Chevy coupe, and we had a car big enough for our family. We found a place to rent on the corner of Fourth Street and Walnut Avenue in downtown Hutchinson. This was where we lived when Steven started kindergarten. At 8:45 a.m., I would watch Steven walk out our back door into an alley, then into the schoolyard. At noon, I would watch him walk back home and eat his lunch, and the boys would have a nap. Ronda was born at St. Elizabeth's Catholic Hospital on December 27, 1957.

In March 1958, Carl found out he had been recommended for officer candidate school in Newport,

Rhode Island. We knew we didn't have the money to live in Newport, Rhode Island. Carl was pretty sure his next orders would be for the West Coast. Carl called my mother in California and told her he would pay all expenses for her to come to Kansas and help me drive our family back to California. We could also spend a couple of weeks in Arkansas, and she could visit her family. Mom agreed but was afraid to fly. She came by train and brought my brother, Ken, with her. He was now sixteen and didn't want to be called Royce anymore. On April 1, 1958, the moving van came; and our furniture was put in storage somewhere. Carl drove us to Clinton, Arkansas. After a couple of days, I took Carl to the bus station in Clinton and kissed him goodbye, and he left for Newport, Rhode Island. He would be in Newport for three months.

We stayed in Arkansas for two weeks, then I drove to Campbell, California. I had enough money for an apartment, but before I had a chance to look for one, my dad wanted to borrow $200. My mother knew I had money on me. My dad said he could pay me back in two days. Two days later, he said he couldn't pay me back but I could stay with them for three months for nothing and we would be even. I had no choice.

Each time that I stayed with my parents, I bought all the food and did all the cooking. Steven finished kindergarten at Rosemary Lane School.

Three months later, Carl called from Newport, Rhode Island. He had finished officer candidate school and was now Lieutenant Carl William Amick. He would be driving to San Diego with three other OCS graduates. He wanted me to drive the Buick to San Diego and meet him there in four days. He had already called the van and storage company, and our furniture was on its way to San Diego. I left my children in Campbell with my mother. I drove to San Diego and checked into the Horton Hotel. I was only there a few hours when Carl knocked on the door. We started looking for a place to rent and found a house on Donna Avenue in the university district. Carl contacted the van and storage people and gave them an address and a date to deliver the furniture. We headed for Campbell to get the children. Within a couple of days, we were settled in. We went to the base and got a nice swing set.

USS Estes (AGC-12)

When Carl graduated from OCS, he was told he would probably be at sea for the next seven years.

His orders were for him to report to the USS *Estes*. The USS *Estes* was the flagship for the Pacific Fleet. Within a couple of weeks, the ship left for six months' tour of duty. September 1958, Steven started first grade at Rolando Park School. Carl told me to look for a house to buy I would put the kids in the car and drive around looking for new housing developments. I found one area I really liked not far from Thirty-Second Street Naval Station. I wrote and told Carl about it. He told me to pick out a lot and put a deposit on it. The lot I chose had a beautiful view of San Diego Bay. I also like that floor plan best. It would be months before that house on Shady Glade Lane was built.

The six months crept by, and the USS *Estes* was returning to San Diego. The boys hadn't changed much, but Ronda's short brown hair had turned into long blonde hair. She was walking. Once the ship was tied up to the dock, we were allowed to go aboard. I was talking to a lady. Her husband was also an officer aboard the USS *Estes*. Her husband came down the steps to tell me Carl had duty and could not leave the ship that day and I was to go to the wardroom with the children and Carl would visit us later. The officer picked up Ronda and started up the steps. I managed to get the three boys up the steps. I followed him to the wardroom. The stewards had baked cookies for the children, including ours. There was probably a dozen children there. Ronda was walking and carrying her orange juice bottle tucked under her arm. She was trying to visit and talk to everyone, but you couldn't understand what she was saying. After a while, Carl came into the wardroom and sat down next to me. The boys came down and kissed their daddy, then went back to their cookies and milk.

Pretty soon, Carl said, "That is the cutest little girl. I wonder whom she belongs to?"

I said, "Carl, that's Ronda."

He thought trying to bring all four children with me was too much and that I had left Ronda with a babysitter. We had a nice long visit. Then I took the children home. I went back the next morning and got Carl. I took him to see the housing development and the lot I had put the deposit on. He liked it. The price of that house was $11,050. It had three bedrooms and one and a half bath.

June 1959, within a couple of weeks, the USS *Estes* was going into dry dock in Long Beach, California, for repairs. Carl wanted us with him, so we put our furniture in storage and moved into the temporary housing in Long Beach. Grandma's box came with me. Carl had bought an old Hudson as a second car for me to drive. Now that he was taking the Buick to the base every day, he wanted me to take the kids out and do things. I did laundry one day, and when I was ready to go home, I couldn't get the Hudson started. I kept going out and trying to start it. Couple of hours later, it finally started. Carl checked it out that night but couldn't find anything wrong. Couple of days later, I decided to take the children to a park.

I asked Carl, "What should I do if I can't get it started to come home?"

He replied, "Call me!" and gave me his number at the base.

We went to the park, had a good time, and started home. I came to a red light, and while I was sitting there, the Hudson died. When the light turned green and after some honking, men in cars behind me pushed me through the intersection and into a gas station on the other side. I called the number Carl had given me and asked for Lieutenant Carl Amick.

A voice on the other end of the phone said, "I'm sorry. He's in a meeting."

I said, "GET HIM OUT!"

Later Carl showed up, and the Hudson still wouldn't start. Carl told me to take the Buick and take the children back to our apartment after that. Carl drove the Hudson to the base, and I had the Buick. He couldn't get the Hudson on the base. He didn't have a sticker, but there was a large parking area just outside the gate. Then he could take a shuttle to where he needed to be. After the Hudson sat there all day, it started up without a problem.

While we were in Long Beach, we took the children to Knott's Berry Farm and Disneyland. While we were at Disneyland, Richard got lost. Carl and Steven were in line for a ride. I took Richard, Eugene, and Ronda for ice cream a few feet away. Richard walked into a booth where they were selling tickets. I walked to the lost children's department and described Richard. They told me where to find him. He was just a few feet from us.

September 1959, now it's time to move back to San Diego and move into our new home on Shady Glade Lane. I drove the Buick. Carl drove the Hudson. We were disappointed to find out our house was not ready. There had been a plumber strike, and now it would be two more months. We found a furnished place on B Street near Golden Hill Park. It was a big two-story house. We rented the downstairs. A family from Samoa rented the upstairs. Out came Grandma Bessie's box. The grammar school was just a block up the street. Richard started kindergarten. I would watch Steven and Richard walk to school, then go back outside at noon and watch. Richard walked back home. There was a puppy in the yard next door that would run up to Richard. It terrified him. Both Carl and I were dog lovers. As soon as we got in our new home on Shady Glade Lane and got a fence, we needed to get a dog.

Carl had worked on the Hudson and didn't have any trouble with it. One day, he was changing oil in the Buick, and I needed to run to the grocery store. I got in the Hudson. A couple of the boys got in with me, and we went to the store. On the way back, I stopped at a red light in front of the fire department.

I started praying, "Please, Lord, don't let this car die on me."

About that time, the siren at the fire department started up. The doors flew open, and the Hudson died. The firemen had to come and push me out of the way to get the fire engine out of the garage. It was too far to walk back to the house. We sat in the Hudson for over an hour, and finally, it started.

When we got back to the house, Carl asked, "What took you so long?"

At that point, that was not the right thing to say. I threw the keys on the kitchen table and said I would never drive that car again. A few days later, Carl had driven the Hudson to the base. When he came home that evening, he was driving an older-model Jeep station wagon. I fell in love with the Jeep.

Now it was finally time to move into our new house on Shady Glade Lane. We arrived that morning waiting for the final inspection. Other families were sitting in their cars waiting for the same thing. Our moving van was supposed to arrive that afternoon. We walked around and met our new neighbors—Inez and Bill Bryan, Walter and Ann DuBois, and Arturo and Bea Carrillo. The inspectors left, and we could finally walk inside. We were standing in our backyard looking out on San Diego Bay.

We heard the boys yelling, "Mom! The movers are here."

The house had three bedrooms, one and a half bath, and a big eat in kitchen. The sliding doors in the large living room looked out on San Diego Bay. We didn't have to make a house payment the first month, so we used the money to put in a covered patio off the living room. We had a two-car garage. The back door of the garage opened onto the patio. There was a chain-link fence running along the back of our yard. Carl talked to the neighbors on both sides, and they would go fifty-fifty on a five-foot red-wood fence. Carl would do the work.

The two-car garage was wide enough to have shelving on one side and my washing machine on the other side and still have room for two cars in the middle. Carl built some shelving, and that was where we set Grandma Bessie's box. Second item in the garage was the wooden chest we used as a toy box, and now Ronda was riding Nong Nong. A lady came by offering accordion lessons, and Steven wanted to do that. Steven and Richard would be attending Freeze Elementary School.

One beautiful Saturday, we took a drive out in backcountry San Diego. We stopped at a fruit stand. There was a sign in the window: "Free puppies." There was a pretty little dog running around. We were told she was the mother.

Carl told the young man standing there, "If you have a male puppy, we will take it."

The young man crawled under the porch and brought out a small, fluffy ball of beige. The children named him Rocky because of the rocks on the hills around us. If the little dog we saw running around was Rocky's mother, his father would've had to be a Great Dane. Rocky grew into a big dog. On nights we had spaghetti for dinner, he could smell it and howl until we took him some. Carl made him a nice doghouse. He wouldn't sleep inside. He slept on top.

USS Hopewell (DD-681)

Carl had orders for the USS *Hopewell*, a destroyer stationed at Thirty-Second Street Naval Station. On Monday mornings, the destroyers would leave San Diego Bay and go on maneuvers. They would return on Friday, about 4:00 p.m. My binoculars stayed on top of the TV. Carl worked in the engine room. He arranged for the *Hopewell* to send a puff of white smoke, a puff of black smoke, and a puff of white smoke as they came around the bend at Point Loma. He knew I would be watching. That was my signal to put the kids in the Buick and go down and pick up Daddy.

Eugene was our sickest child. About every month, I had to run him to Balboa Naval Hospital. I was told he needed to have his tonsils and adenoids removed. He was put on the waiting list. Each time I took him back to the hospital, I was told he was still on the list, but nothing happened. Captain Morrissey was captain of the USS *Hopewell*. Every month, his wife held a luncheon for the officers' wives. I never attended the luncheons/

The *Graf Spee*, a German ship, came into San Diego Harbor. The USS *Hopewell* sponsored a dinner for its officers, one of the few times we got a babysitter. At the dinner, Mrs. Morrissey, the captain's wife, sat next to me. First time I had met her, she asked why I never attended the luncheons. I explained I had four children under the age of eight and my youngest son was sick a lot. She asked why he was sick. I told her he needed to have his tonsils and adenoids removed and had been on the waiting list at Balboa Naval Hospital for over two years. We had a nice dinner.

A few days later, the phone rang. It was Balboa Naval Hospital asking me to bring Eugene in. When I got to the hospital, I was taken to the head surgeon's office. He examined Eugene, then filled out paperwork for me to go to Spring Valley Medical Center to have Eugene's tonsils and adenoids removed. He then told me his next-door neighbor was the captain of the USS *Hopewell* and the captain's wife asked for this favor. That was when I realized it was not what you know but who you know.

I drove to Spring Valley Medical Center, just down the road from our house. It was a Seventh-Day Adventist hospital. I got all the paperwork done. Carl took a few days' leave to be home with the other children. I checked Eugene in at 7:30 a.m. the next day. There were two other children ahead of him. They were sitting in the hallway on their hospital beds, waiting for their turn to go into surgery. Eugene thought this was a big adventure and kept telling me I could go. Finally it was his turn. They wheeled him into the operating room. By now, it was lunchtime. I decided to find the cafeteria and get something to eat. It was a big hospital, and it took me a while to find the cafeteria. I saw something that looked like meat loaf. So I ordered the meat loaf. That was when I was told Seventh-day Adventists do not eat meat. What I saw was walnut roast. I got a slice, along with some vegetables; took my tray; and sat down at a table. Before I could take a bite, one of the other mothers came in and said my little boy was screaming, "Mommy! Mommy! Mommy!" I hurried back upstairs. I still wonder what walnut roast tasted like.

Later the doctor came into Eugene's room and said he had never seen tonsils and adenoids that big and a child that young. They kept Eugene overnight, and I stayed with him. We were so glad to have this done before he started school.

In the fall of 1960, the children would be attending Freeze Elementary School. Eugene was starting kindergarten. He would only go half a day. My best friend, Inez, and her husband, John, lived across the street. Their little girl Danni was also in kindergarten. Eugene and Danni walked home together.

The USS *Hopewell* left for six months in the Pacific. It was never six months. It was more like seven or eight. They would have to leave a month early because the ship on line had problems and needed to go into port, or they would have to stay on the line a month longer because the ship that was due to relieve them couldn't get underway for one reason or another. I used my binoculars and watched the destroyers leave San Diego Bay.

I tried to stay busy. We had sold the bunkbeds and the single bed we had for the boys and bought two sets of trundle beds. Steven and Richard shared one bedroom. Eugene and Ronda shared another. I made bedspreads and curtains for the children's rooms. I wallpapered one wall in my big kitchen. I saw an ad for canopy bed frame. I bought the bed frame and made a bedspread matching the canopy top and curtains for our room. I made Ronda's clothes. I knitted a couple of afghans. We also got a parakeet.

Dinner was always at 6:00 p.m. Whether Carl was home or not, the boys would come home from school, change into their play clothes, and join the neighborhood kids out front. After dinner, they weren't allowed to go back out front. We watched TV. We played board games and enjoyed our backyard with our beautiful view.

In the spring of 1961, the USS *Hopewell* returned to San Diego. We were on the dock to meet it. Later we went to a nice restaurant for dinner. Going out to eat was a treat for our children. Many times people would come to our table and comment on how well behaved our children were.

Within a couple of weeks, the USS *Hopewell* was going into dry dock for three months in San Francisco. While the *Hopewell* was there, Carl would be attending engineering school. Carl wanted us with him. A navy lieutenant, a friend of Carl's, wanted to rent our house furnished. We couldn't take Rocky. He was too big. We took him to the animal shelter and told them what a good dog he was and left two big bags of dog food.

Grandma Bessie's box went into the back of the Buick. Carl drove the Jeep station wagon with two children and the parakeet. I followed in the Buick with the other two children. After a couple of miles, I started honking the horn. Carl pulled over and came back to see what I wanted. I told him he needed to roll his window. The poor little parakeet's wings were flapping like crazy, and at that rate, it would never survive the trip.

The children and I stopped at my parents' house in Campbell. Carl took the Buick and went on to the ship. He put an ad in the paper looking for us a place. The next day, a lady called. She had a two-bedroom apartment. We took it. There was a foldout couch in the living room that made a bed. That was where Carl and I slept. It was located on Ramsell Street in San Francisco. The houses were built side by side. You only had windows on the front and the back in the kitchen and bathroom. There were skylights. There was room for two cars in the garage, which was under the house. You parked one in front of the other. The boys attended Jose Ortega School. They would walk down the hill, across the street, up the hill, and into the schoolyard. I stood on the front sidewalk and watch them go to and come home from school. On Friday nights, I would fix a big tamale pie and a big salad, and we would drive to Campbell. That way, my parents could visit their grandchildren.

Carl finished engineering school. The *Hopewell* came out of dry dock, and we headed back to our home in San Diego. A few months later, the USS *Hopewell* needed to go into dry dock at Mare Island near San Francisco, this time for major repairs. Carl put an ad in the San Francisco paper looking for a house to rent. He found one in Colma, California. This time, the movers had an address to deliver our furniture to. The boys would ride the city bus to Daniel Webster Elementary School. We signed a year's lease.

The day we moved in, the neighbors across the street came over and introduced themselves. They were Reggie and Marge Oakley. Reggie worked for the *San Francisco Examiner*. Marge's grandfather had been prime minister of Canada. Marge had been married before and had a daughter, Judy. Reggie and Marge had a son, Brad. Brad sold his Australian racing bike to Steven for $10. In just a short time, we became good friends.

You could tell the house had oil heat. When the family before us took their pictures off the wall, you could see the outline of each picture. All the walls needed washing. I got some TSP and started washing walls. Next I had to cut off some curtains and add lace to other curtains to make them fit the windows.

My brother, Ken, had gotten mad at his girl-friend, Vonda, and joined the navy. After doing his boot camp in San Diego, he was to leave San Francisco International Airport heading for Japan. I fixed a nice lunch for my mom, Dad, Ken, and

Vonda. After lunch, Carl drove them to the airport. They stayed with Ken a few hours, then the sailors were taken somewhere. When they returned to our house, they said they didn't see Ken get on a plane. Mom, Dad, and Vonda returned to Campbell.

At one time, my father had a business partner named Woody Wilson. My father was always verbally abusive to my mother. He made her quit her job at the cannery to be his secretary. If she did the least thing wrong, he would wait until there were men in the office and then tell them about it. Many times, she would leave the office in tears and go to the café next door. Woody was kindhearted and would follow her and buy her a cup of coffee. Woody was separated from his wife. The year before, he had moved to Reno, Nevada, and was buying a Seven Seas gas station. That evening, when my mom and dad returned home from being with Ken at the airport, Woody was in Campbell visiting his son. My dad went somewhere. Woody went into the garage at his son's home and called my mother. His wife was listening. Later that evening, Woody's wife called my dad and told him everything she heard Woody and my mother were talking about. My father threw a fit. The shoe was on the other foot now. My father had girl friends that my mother knew about. My mother got hold of Woody and put a few things into a bag, and they took off for Nevada. My mother filed for divorce. Woody's wife refused to give him a divorce. There was a big insurance policy she wanted. In six weeks, her divorce was final. She lived with Woody in Nevada for about a year. My brother, Ken, didn't fly to Japan that night. The navy put the sailors up in a hotel in San Francisco. On Saturday morning, my brother called home to tell my parents where he was. My dad told him that Mom had run off with Woody. Ken left the hotel and hitchhiked back to Campbell. When he got to the house, he and my dad got into a big argument. Ken told my dad he was going AWOL and left the house. My dad called us. He wanted to talk to Carl. We got in the car and headed for Campbell. It was only a forty-minute drive. We got to the house. The kids and I got out of the car. Carl took off looking for my brother. About two hours later, Carl returned to the house with my brother, Ken. Carl found him walking down the highway heading for Vonda's house. My dad told Ken he would pay to fly Vonda to Japan. He would also send Ken money each month for an apartment in Japan.

We drove back to Colma. The kids and I got out at our house, and Carl took Ken back to the hotel and told him to stay there. The next morning, Ken called our house. They were getting on the plane for Japan. He wanted to apologize to Carl for all the trouble he caused. Two weeks later, Vonda married someone else.

A few days later, Wednesday, at breakfast, Carl asked what my plans were for the day.

I told him, "Now that all the walls have been washed, I'm going to unpack those barrels in the garage so we can get the car in there."

The barrels were filled with my good china and glassware. About ten o'clock, I heard the phone ring. It was Carl. He asked what I was doing.

I replied, "I'm unpacking those barrels in the garage."

He said, "Don't unpack anymore. Repack what you took out this morning. The movers will be there Friday at 8:00 a.m. I have emergency orders back to San Diego to go aboard the USS *Rogers*, another destroyer."

We called the landlord. He came over and was pleased that all the walls had been washed. When we lived on Donna Avenue, one of my neighbors, Linda Evans, was a realtor. I called her and told her our situation. I needed a house in my neighborhood so my children could attend their school.

USS Rogers (DD-876)

She called back later. She found a house on our street, across the street and three houses down. It was for sale, but I could rent it month to month.

Judy, the girl across the street, was having problems with her stepfather. Her mother asked me to take her to San Diego with us. Carl said okay. Marge filled out papers, making us her guardian.

The movers arrived at 8:00 a.m. Friday. By Saturday night, we were in the rental house just down the street from our home. We got up Sunday morning, and Judy's boyfriend was lying out on our front porch. I don't know what happened, but we never saw him again. Everything was okay for about a month, then Judy started cutting school and not wanting to get up in the mornings. The USS *Rogers* was getting ready to go to sea. Carl didn't want Judy to give me problems. We called Marge, explained the situation, put Judy on a bus, and sent her back to Colma.

On Monday morning, our children went back to school but not Freeze Elementary School. They were still building homes in our neighborhood, and a new school had been built. Now they would be attending Boone Elementary. It wasn't any farther for

our children to walk. They just walked in the opposite direction. Steven was in fifth grade. Richard was
in third grade, and Eugene was in second grade. Carl
and I attended the PTA meetings. They were starting a new Boy Scout pack. Both Steven and Richard
wanted to be Cub Scouts. Eugene wasn't old enough.
They needed den mother's and committeemen. I
became a den mother and Carl a committeeman. I
had my two sons plus eight other boys.

When Carl reported to the USS *Rogers*, he
was told why he had received emergency orders. He
replaced a missing naval officer. A year later, they
would find the missing officer's body in backcountry
San Diego. Along with his navy ID, they found razor
blades. He had committed suicide. He was from
Hawaii and of Japanese descent. His naval career was
not going well.

On December 1, 1961, the USS *Rogers* left
for a six-month tour of duty. Two months later, the
sailor renting our house flunked out of school. They
wanted out of their lease. No problem. Within the
week, they moved out of my house, and I was moving back in. I rented a U-Haul. John Bryan and his
cousin Albert helped me move back into my own
home. The kids and I wanted to eat all our meals out
on the patio. Years earlier, we had purchased a picnic

table and two benches. Now I couldn't get enough of my view of San Diego Bay and watching the ships coming and going. I enjoyed being a den mother. At one PTA meeting, the pack leader said they were looking for a place to store items to be sold at flea markets. They needed to raise money for the new Boy Scout pack. I wrote Carl. He said they could use our garage. Our driveway was wide enough for both cars to sit outside. In no time, our garage was full of flea market items. Early on Saturday mornings, men would show up, load items onto a couple of pickup trucks, and go to the flea markets.

On Saturday nights, they would return with what they didn't sell. During the week, they would bring in donated items to add to what was in the garage.

I had not been back in my own home very long when I got bad news from my friend Inez. John had lost his job at Ryan Aeronautical He was going to Torrance, near Los Angeles, and stay with his mother while he looked for a job up there. Inez, Danni, and John Jr. were going to stay in their house until she got evicted. John's cousin Albert used to visit a lot, but now John wanted Albert to stay with Inez. John didn't want her alone with two little children and no car. John and Inez had recently purchased a new TV and a freezer. After missing a couple of payments, the TV was repossessed. I took over the payments on the freezer. John and Albert moved it into my garage, near my kitchen door. After John left for Torrance, most evenings after dinner, Inez, Albert, and the children would come over to watch TV and do jigsaw puzzles. I kept my jigsaw puzzles on a big board that I would slide under the couch during the day. I enjoyed the company. After a couple of months, John found a job and a place to live near Torrance. The moving van came and got their furniture. I was really going to miss them.

Bea and Arturo Carrillo lived across the street next to John and Inez. Arturo was a navy cook. He never went aboard a ship. He worked for an admiral in San Diego. Their mama cat had kittens. They were born in the stationary tub next to Bea's washing machine. She showed them to me when they were about two weeks old. One day, she came over to have tea with me. She brought a cute little black kitten with a little white under its chin and a little bit of white on its belly. I really didn't want a kitten. After she left, I thought about it and decided to take the kitten back to her house. I told her I didn't want the kitten.

She said, "That's okay. Just put it back in the garage with the others. I stepped into her garage and started to put the kitten in the stationary tub. I was shocked. She had put the plug in the stationary tub and filled it with water, and the other kittens had drowned. We named the kitten Herman.

Ann and Walter Dubois lived two houses down. Walter worked for the railroad. They had two teen-age daughters, Maureen and Barbara.

Carl had taken me to the officers' club at Thirty-Second Street a few times for dinner. On Thursday evenings, they had bingo. Carl knew I loved bingo and was very lucky. If you ate dinner there on Thursday nights, you would get a free bingo card. Cards were normally a dollar apiece. At halftime, the cards went on sale half price, 50¢. Before the USS *Rogers* left port, Carl suggested I have one of the DuBois girls babysit on Thursday nights and for me to go play bingo at the officers' club. The children were older now, and I would be home by 9:00 p.m., which was their bedtime.

Ann Dubois loved bingo and would go with me. We would have dinner and get our free card. She would buy nine more. At halftime, I would buy one card for 50¢. She would buy ten more for $5. I won more times with my two cards than she did with her twenty. I think the problem was she had too many cards and couldn't watch them all. She got very upset with me. She suggested I share my winnings with her fifty-fifty and she would share hers with me. No way! I paid her daughter to babysit. I drove her to the base. She couldn't get in the officers' club without me, and now she thought I should give her half of my winnings. As I said, I'm very lucky. After a few months, I had won all the small appliances I needed. I opened a charge account at Walker Scott department store. I started taking the $10 Walker Scott gift certificates when I won at bingo. Just before Easter, I won the $50 jackpot. The boys got new sport coat jackets, and Ronda got a new dress. One day at Walker Scott department store, they were having a sale on furs. I saw a Russian squirrel that I liked. It was $79. I put it on my charge account and paid it off with my bingo winnings.

June 1962, the USS *Rogers* came back home. The kids and I went down to meet the ship. Later we went to a nice restaurant and had dinner, and again a couple came to our table and commented on how well behaved our children were. Going out to eat was a treat, and they were always on their best behavior. After we got home, we were watching KOGO channel 7 news in San Diego, and there was Ronda and the boys waving at the ship as it pulled up to the dock.

I saw an ad for a Doughboy aboveground swimming pool. It was fifteen feet across, five feet deep in the middle, and four feet deep around the edges. We bought it. There was room in our side yard to set it up. The boys loved it. Ronda was a little afraid at first, but it didn't take her long to enjoy it. The Cub Scouts could play in the pool after our meetings, with a note from their mother. Carl took my Cub Scouts on a field trip to the USS *Rogers*.

Christmas 1962, one of the few Christmases Carl was home with us, turned into a nightmare. My father called the week before Christmas and wanted to know if my mother was coming to visit us at Christmas. My brother, Ken, was still stationed in Japan. My father said he wanted to see the kids. He said, if my mother was coming for Christmas, he would wait and come New Year's. I called her in Nevada. She said yes. She was coming by bus to San Diego to spend a few days before and after Christmas with the kids. I called my dad back and told him. A few days later, my mother arrived. The next morning, Christmas Eve, Carl left for the ship. The kids were in the backyard playing. The phone rang. It was my father. He wanted to talk to my mother. He said, if she didn't talk to him, he would just keep calling until she did. She got on the extension in my bedroom. They talked for a couple of hours. When she came out into the kitchen, she was crying. She said my father was flying into San Diego Christmas morning. She had already called Woody, and he was driving down from Nevada. Christmas morning, I got up and started Christmas dinner. Carl drove to the airport and picked up my father. My mother was in Ronda's room and didn't want to come out until Woody got there.

Woody arrived and picked up my mother. They went to Tijuana, Mexico. They were gone all day. My dad sat at the kitchen table and cried about how good he had been to my mother and how badly she had treated him. Finally Carl had all he could take.

He told my father, "You have ruined our Christmas, one of the few Christmases I've got to spend with my family. You never treated her right."

Later in the afternoon, Mom and Woody would return from Tijuana. Mom was too upset to eat. I fixed Woody a plate. My father went out into the backyard and stayed while Woody was in the house. My mother got her things together. Woody brought in Christmas gifts for my children. Then she and Woody left for Nevada. Although my father's plane wouldn't leave till much later that evening, Carl took him to the airport and left him.

A few weeks later, my mother returned to Campbell and remarried my dad. She said, while Dad had her on the phone, Dad said he had gotten a letter from my brother, Ken. Ken said in the letter, when his time in the navy was up, he would stay in Japan and not return to the US because he didn't have a home to come back to. My mother said, although she loved Woody, she loved Ken more. After my brother, Ken, returned home, he told me he never wrote a letter like that.

A few months later, Woody Wilson knocked on my door. He had a gift for me, a little white Chihuahua. Her registered name was Silver Baby, but he called her Pixie. She was the sweetest puppy. He also brought the kids some coconut candy. After that, the kids called it Woody candy. He didn't stay long, just wanted to know how my mother was. In 1986, after my father passed away, Woody and my mother married.

Summer of 1963, Carl had new orders for San Clemente Island. The Boy Scouts would have to find another place to store the flea market items. The pool would have to be drained and disassembled. We rent our house on Shady Glade Lane to Mr. and Mrs.

Jacques. Carl put an ad in the paper, and we found a house on San Anselmo Street in Long Beach, near the airport. Carl would fly to the island on Monday mornings and fly back on Fridays unless he had the duty. He would have duty every fourth weekend. On those weekends, the boys would take turns flying out on Friday nights, spending the weekend with Carl, and flying back home on Monday mornings. I sent their school clothes with them so I could take them straight to school. We never let Ronda go to the island and spent the weekend with her dad. We felt she was too young, and there were no women on the island. The children would be attending Washington Carver School. Ronda would be in kindergarten and go half a day.

We arrived at the house waiting for the movers. We put Herman in the front hall closet along with his food water and litter box to keep him safe. I carried Pixie. After the furniture was all put in place, we opened the hall closet door to let Herman out. He didn't want to come out. After a week, he came out, looked around the living room, and went back in the closet. The next night, he came out, went over, and lay by Steven on the rug as we watched TV. A few more days and he was sleeping with Steven every night.

Now it was time to put the pool up and get it filled. We were not too far from Carl's brother Fred and his children, Donna and Tommy. We wanted them over for a cookout. They arrived, and we had a great time. Fred and Jane were divorced. The children lived with Jane. While Carl was on the island, he had his own lobster traps. Every so often, Carl would call Fred and have him come for dinner, and I would fix lobster. I always broiled a few extra lobsters for Fred to take home with him.

Steven loved to fish. There was a nice little park not far from our house. It had a pond with fish. On Saturday mornings when Carl was home, Steven would get up early and walk to the park. Around noon, I would pack a lunch, and we would all go there to join him. Richard got a toy ship for Christmas. Richard would get on one side of the pond and Eugene on the other, and they would send the ship back and forth. There were white geese on the pond. Ronda would try and catch them. My little dog, Pixie, just loved to run around. One Saturday, Steven caught three little fish. He wanted to bring them home. He put them in a bowl on the sink. We got up Sunday morning, and the fish were gone. There was water splashed all around the bowl.

Steven said, "Herman, what did you do?"

Not long after we moved into the house, a little boy showed up. His name was Billy. He was Ronda's age and in her kindergarten class. He lived on the corner two houses from us. He told his mommy about the nice lady who just moved in. His mother, Sandy, came down to meet me. She was a seamstress, and I made Ronda's clothes. We had a lot in common and would go to the fabric store together and get our materials. We became good friends and spent a lot of time at each other's house. We decided to take our S&H Green Stamps to the redemption center. Carl needed a new briefcase. That morning, we got the children off to school, then we went into downtown Long Beach. I got Carl's briefcase. We came home. I picked up Ronda, went home, and turned on the TV. President John Fitzgerald Kennedy had been assassinated. Carl came home that weekend. We all stayed glued to the TV set. What a sad time.

Steven had spent the weekend with Carl on the island. When I picked him up on Monday morning, he had a note from Carl. It said, "Don't let Steven go to school. He had fallen into a cactus plant on the island and had spent time in the infirmary. He still has stickers in him. They had not gotten them all out." I took Steven home, gave him some aspirin, and put him on the kitchen table under a good light.

I got my magnifying glass and tweezers and proceeded to get the rest of the stickers out. His poor little rump was black and blue. The next time it was Steven's turn to spend the weekend with his dad, he couldn't wait to get on that plane.

Carl had been on San Clemente Island for a year. He got new orders. He would be stationed at Pasadena Naval Station. He reported for duty. It was an hour and a half drive from where we live in Long Beach. He didn't have time to look for us a place to live. One morning, he took the Jeep station wagon to work and left me the Buick. I told the boys, if I wasn't there when they came in from school, to just stay in the house and watch TV until I got home. I put Pixie in the car and picked Ronda up from kindergarten. She only went half a day. I had a map of the Pasadena area. I made a circle on the map. As soon as I entered the circle, I started stopping at grocery stores and looking at their bulletin boards. After a dozen stops and a few phone calls, I found a listing for a house in Covina. I used the pay phone to call the owner. The house on Starcrest was still available. I called Carl. He would leave work early and meet me and the owner there. It was on a cul-de-sac. The school was only half block away. The house had four bedrooms and two baths with a large fenced-in backyard. It was only a twenty-minute drive to Carl's office in Pasadena. We signed a lease.

There were only a few days left of the school year. As soon as school was over in Long Beach, we moved to Covina. Karen, my next-door neighbor, came over to introduce herself. We discovered we shared a birthday, October 11. She had three children, two boys and a baby girl. The oldest boy was Ronda's age. She wanted to go to work and asked if I would babysit for her. I said okay. She found a job at Kentucky Fried Chicken. I watched her children from 8:00 a.m. to 5:00 p.m. five days a week. The first thing I bought with my babysitting money was a combination hi-fi stereo / radio / record player with a nineteen-inch color television set for my children. There were only a few colored programs. One of them was *The Wonderful World of Disney*. That program alone made it worth it.

One Saturday, we decided to put up the pool. We got it up and started filling it. When it was about half full, Steven got in and was playing around. The pool had been used many years before we bought it. Steven's foot put a hole in the liner, and we flooded the backyard of three neighbors. No damage was done. The family next door that I babysit for had put grass seed in their backyard a couple of years before.

No grass ever came up. After we flooded their backyard, they had grass. A few weeks later, Eugene went through a gate into the neighbors' backyard to talk to their oldest boy. He tripped over a Rain Bird and split the top of his foot wide open. Because of the high grass, he couldn't see the watering device.

He started screaming, "Mommy! Mommy! Mommy!"

It was on a Saturday, and Carl was home. I wrapped his foot in a towel, and we headed for the nearest naval hospital. He had sixteen stitches in his foot. He was not allowed to stand on it. We had a roll-around TV stand. He used that as a wheelchair. Carl used the pool liner to make a tent, and now the boys could camp out in the backyard.

Carl wanted to go camping. He got a tent from the base. We bought six sleeping bags and a camp stove and boarded Pixie in a nearby vet clinic. Herman would be fine at the house. We went to Leo Carrillo State Park at Malibu. Carl couldn't figure out how to get our tent set up. He thought they had forgotten to give us the poles. We found a large bush we could crawl under for a little privacy. We spent a week there. As soon as we got home, the children and I walked across the schoolyard to get Pixie. I was told she had not eaten that whole week. She thought we had abandoned her. I was wearing a lacy blouse. She was so excited to see us. I tried to carry her, but her nail shredded my blouse. We were laughing. I put her on the ground, and she ran circles all over the schoolyard. The next time we left her, she did fine. She knew we would come back and get her.

Carl bought me a stackable washer and dryer. I had never had a dryer before. Most places we live didn't have room for a dryer. The next thing I bought with my babysitting money was a large maple dining room table and six chairs. I still have that table in my dining room.

At the grocery store one day, I ran into my old friend Margie Oakley, our neighbor from Colma. Reggie now worked for the *Los Angeles Times*. They lived in San Dimas, not too far from Covina. I invited them over for dinner. Reggie brought some golf clubs. He was trying to get Carl into golfing. It wasn't Carl's thing. He would rather spend time doing things with our children. At dinner, I asked Marge about her daughter, Judy. She said, when Judy returned to Colma, she couldn't do anything with her. She finally shipped her off to her father in Canada.

Joyce, a lady who lived across the street, owned horses and gave riding lessons. I met her at the bakery wagon that came up our street every morning at

10:00 a.m. She was also a tea drinker. We would take turns, along with my neighbor Gayle, going to each other's homes to have our tea/coffee and share our cookies. Joyce had two dogs. They would follow her when she came to my house, and then they wanted in. They were well behaved, and Pixie loved the company. They would clean out her food bowl. She didn't care. I had never seen that breed of dog before, and I fell in love with them. They were Australian shepherds.

Carl had sixty days' leave on the books. He wanted to use some of it up. He made arrangements to rent one of the cabins on San Clemente Island for the family for a week. Ronda and I had never been there. We boarded Pixie at the vet and flew to the island. Carl took us for a tour of the island. There were wild goats left there by the Spaniards. We saw the San Clemente National Forest, which consisted of three trees, the only trees on the island. Three different times, we got on a boat and went deep-sea fishing. It was a wonderful vacation.

Our cat, Herman, had learned how to yank the screens off of the bedroom windows to get in. Carl fixed the screens in the bedrooms where they couldn't be yanked off, then he took off the screen on the window over the kitchen sink and set a large trash can under the window. Now Herman could come and go as he wished. It wasn't unusual to get up in the morning and find a dead gopher next to my washing machine.

Herman was a black cat with a little white under his chin. I had made Steven a birthday cake the night before his birthday. I set it on the kitchen table in a plastic cake dish with the plastic cover. It was a chocolate cake with white icing. During the night, another cat had followed Herman through the window. They had fought on the kitchen table. There were bits of chocolate cake and white icing along with a lot of white hair. Since Herman was black, it had to belong to the other cat. The kids helped me clean up the mess. I baked Steven another cake.

About once a month, Carl had to drive to China Lake, California. It was almost a deserted road. On one trip, as he was driving home, he saw a large package lying in the middle of the road. He got out and picked it up and put it in the back of the Buick. It was a very expensive television antenna. We were surprised to see how much better our reception was.

One night, Carl came home with a naval officer's tuxedo. It needed to have stripes sewn on the sleeves. We were invited to the world premiere of *In Harm's Way*, a motion picture starring John Wayne and Kirk Douglas. I sewed the stripes on his sleeves and bought myself a fancy new dress. Gayle baby-sat for us. We were taken to the Pantages Chinese Theater in Los Angeles by navy bus. The bus was filled with naval officers and their wives. The red carpet was rolled out for us with all the fanfare you see on television at a movie premiere. After viewing the movie, we were invited upstairs to a reception and met some of the stars that came to the premiere. We met Aldo Ray, Sally Field, Tab Hunter, Carolyn Jones, and many others.

Joyce, my friend across the street, wanted to go to San Francisco to the Cow Palace and watch some of her students compete. She would leave on Friday afternoon and return on Monday. She asked if I could watch her two boys Friday night, Saturday night, and Sunday night. Her husband would be home during the day, but he worked nights. She didn't want the boys in the house alone. Joyce's dog didn't know where she was. They practically lived at my house while she was gone. The more time I spent with those dogs, the more I fell in love with them.

Christmas 1964, we drive the Buick station wagon to San Jose to see my parents. Carl gave me a package. It had black lacy underwear and a green key case. The underwear didn't surprise me, but the key case did. Later I would find out the key case was the same color as a four-door 1964 Buick sedan. Carl had traded in our Buick station wagon. An employee of the car lot was taking the 1964 Buick for it to be washed, and he scraped the fender. It had to be repaired. Carl would have to wait a few more days to surprise me.

On New Year's Day 1965, we attended a football game at the Rose Bowl in Pasadena between Michigan Spartans and Oregon Wolverines. A naval officer at Pasadena graduated from Michigan. Carl was offered tickets to the game. We would sit on the Michigan side. My friend Gayle would babysit. Carl was a big football fan and really enjoyed the game.

We had planned to go to sunrise service on Easter morning. On Saturday, we got a phone call. Carl's father had passed away in West Virginia. Carl called Fred and told him we would pick him up and drive him to LA International Airport and they would fly to West Virginia together. When Carl and Fred arrived in West Virginia, plans had to be made. Carl's mother, Lena, could not live alone on the farm with an invalid daughter. It was decided. Carl would take a month's leave and stay with his mother. Fred would return to California, get rid of everything he owned, put what he wanted to keep in the back of his pickup truck, and drive back to West Virginia. Carl's mother, Lena, valued the farm at $6,000. Fred would get the farm. Each of the other boys—Ray, Robert, and Carl—would each get $2,000. Fred returned to West Virginia, and Carl came home.

We took the kids to Huntington Beach quite a ways from Covina. When we were ready to leave the beach and go home, Carl walked on ahead to get the car so I wouldn't have to walk so far.

All of a sudden, all four kids started yelling, "Our Buick! Our Buick!"

The year before, when we lived in Long Beach, we had talked about trading the Buick in but decided not to. Instead we had it painted a beautiful Chinese green and decided to keep it a while longer. There was no other 1957 Buick station wagon painted that color. I walked up to the car and explained to the couple that my children had grown up in the back of that car and, if they looked in the glove compartment, they would see paperwork with the name Carl Amick on it. They started laughing and said, yes, they had already seen the paperwork.

Later Carl had to fly to Washington DC before returning home; stopped off in Charleston, West Virginia; rented a car; and visited his mother and Fred. One day, Carl and Fred went looking at farms for sale. They found one in Summers County, near Elton, 176 acres for $1,800. It had a house that was in shambles and a barn and a steep hillside with an apple orchard on top. Carl bought it.

One evening in mid-November, the phone rang. Carl answered and was told he had orders to Portland, Oregon. They wanted him there yesterday. He was to take command of the USS *Patapsco* (AOG-1). The ship was in dry dock at Swan Island in Portland, Oregon. He was told it would only take three months to put the ship back in the water. Carl didn't want to move the children to Portland for three months. We decided I would stay in Covina. Carl put his sea chest in the back of the Jeep station and headed for Portland. Later that evening, he called me. The Jeep station wagon had broken down before he reached the bay area. He was told what the problem was, and had he been home, he could have fixed it. There was a used-car lot next to the gas station he had pulled into. They had a Rambler. They would trade for the Jeep, and his sea chest would fit in the back of the Rambler. Instead of a gearshift, it had pushbuttons on the dashboard.

Carl arrived in Portland, Oregon, and went out to Swan Island to look at the ship. It had been torn down to where nothing was left but the hull. After he was there a couple of days and talked to the engineers, he knew it would be a lot longer than three months to get the *Patapsco* seaworthy. He called me and told me he didn't want to be away from me and the children any more than he had to be. He wanted me to call the movers and put everything in storage and he would find us a furnished house in Portland.

Two days before Thanksgiving, the movers picked up our furniture. I drove the children with our dog, Pixie, and our cat, Herman, to my parents' house in San Jose. Carl did not want me driving in Northern California by myself. He would fly into San Jose Airport and meet me.

After my mother and father remarried, he bought her a brand-new home. It was mostly for show. They didn't eat in the new kitchen. They had a kitchen table, chairs, electric frypan, coffee maker, and toaster in the attached garage where they fixed and ate their breakfast. Lunch and dinner were eaten in restaurants. There was a stationary tub next to the washing machine in the garage. That was where my mother washed their breakfast dishes. When we visited, my boys slept in the garage on a rollaway bed, along with our dog and cat.

I had offered to pay for us to go to a restaurant and eat on Thanksgiving Day, but my father wanted me to fix a home-cooked Thanksgiving dinner at their house. He wanted all the leftovers. I went to the grocery store early that morning and got a nice-sized turkey, dressing, cranberry sauce, green beans, sweet potatoes, hot rolls, pitted black olives (we always have to have black olives), celery, cream cheese, aluminum foil, and three frozen pies. I came home and started preparing Thanksgiving dinner. Since my mother had never turned on her new double oven, I had to go to the neighbor next door and had her show me how to turn it on. My mother called my brother, Ken, and invited them to dinner. Ken had gotten married; and now I could meet his wife, Karen, and their baby son, Kenny. Later that evening, I picked Carl up at the San Jose Airport, and Carl ate his Thanksgiving dinner.

Early the next morning, we headed for Portland, not knowing what to expect. Grandma Bessie's box was in the trunk. Carl had rented a big two-story house at 44 Northwest McLean Boulevard. The park across the street had the statue of Sacagawea. The family had listed their home with the realtor and were supposed to be out by Thanksgiving. They were spending the winter in Hawaii. When we got to Portland, they were still in their home. We found a motel with a kitchenette. Thank God for Grandma

Bessie's box. On Monday, we took the children and enrolled them in the school they would attend until we moved into the house. Carl would drop them off at school on his way to Swan Island. Later the bus would pick them up in front of our house and, after school, drop them off at the end of the street at the intersection.

On December 3, 1965, we took the ferry up Puget Sound to Seattle, Washington. We had lunch on the ferry. That afternoon, Carl would be the guest speaker at the recommissioning of the USS *Jouett* (DLG/CG) in Seattle. Its commanding officer would be Captain Robert Hayes. He graduated from OCS with Carl and was one of the officers in the car when they drove from Newport, Rhode Island, to San Diego.

We took the children to Mount Hood. Carl and I took the ski lift to the top and rode back down again. It was a beautiful sunny day, but it still had lots of snow. The boys took off their winter coats and used them like sleds.

At Christmas, Steven got a chemistry set. The house had a nice big basement. Steven put his chemistry set down there. Every time I heard a bang, I would run to the basement door and make sure he was okay. Richard built a fort under the stairs. The house was sitting on the steep hill. You could reach out the basement window and touch the ground. We left one basement window open just enough so our cat, Herman, could go out.

Starting the first of the year, I had a calendar on the wall in the kitchen. When the sun shone, I would mark the calendar. From January until June, when we left, there were only fourteen days that the sun shone. It might not have been raining on those days, but it was cloudy. I got very depressed. Carl started bringing someone home for lunch about once a week. That worked. I would fix a nice lunch and have someone to eat with. Within a few more days, two more officers arrived. They had orders to the *Patapsco* and had their wives with them. I taught myself to knit and crochet when Steven was a baby. Andrea and Sally, the two wives I had just met, wanted to learn to knit. Sears was giving free knitting lessons. The three of us signed up. Once a week, after our knitting lessons, we would have lunch. I was feeling better.

One afternoon, Richard did not come home with the others. I got in the Rambler. The kids told me where to turn to follow the bus route. I found Richard walking not far from the house. He had watched the boys in his class go get their jackets out of the cloakroom five minutes before the class would be dismissed. On this day, five minutes before the class would be dismissed, Richard got up with the other boys and got his jacket.

The teacher asked, "What do you think you're doing? You stay after school."

So Richard missed the bus. This teacher also insisted on calling Richard Dick. Richard explained he had never been called Dick and preferred Richard. It didn't matter. The teacher continued to call him Dick. When Carl came home, I told him what happened. He called the school and asked for the teacher's phone number, but they would not give it to him. He lodged a complaint against the teacher. The next morning, he took the children to school, found the teacher, and read him the riot act. He never harassed Richard again and never called him Dick.

The children rode the city bus and didn't sit together. One day, Ronda was not paying attention. The boys got off, and she didn't. Next thing she knew, she was in Downtown Portland. She went up and talked to the bus driver, and he was very mean to her. She was only in second grade. She started crying. Some nice lady gave her a dime. She got off of the bus, got into a phone booth, and called me. I always made sure our children had the phone number where we lived. I put the boys in the Rambler, and we went and picked her up.

Our cat, Herman, disappeared. Normally, when we called him, he would show up in just a matter of minutes. After he was gone, about two months, we gave up hope and closed the basement window. A few weeks later, Carl and I woke up.

The kids were all yelling, "Herman! Herman!"

The kids could hear him, but we couldn't figure out where he was. Finally Carl saw him on the roof over the back kitchen door. We brought him in the house, and he was so skinny. The kids started taking everything out of the refrigerator they thought Herman might eat. He was happy to be back with us.

The boys had a skateboard. It was red and well-worn and had little wings on the side. Ronda was pushing it up the sidewalk when she slipped the skateboard, flew out of her hands, and hit her nose on the sidewalk.

The work on the USS *Patapsco* was being completed. The school year was over. The *Patapsco* was a fuel cargo ship. For Carl's peace of mind, he wanted me in my hometown surrounded by people I knew in case something should happen to him. I wouldn't have to move again. The *Patapsco* would be homeported in Hawaii but would only be there six weeks before they went to Vietnam. Carl didn't want me driving back to San Jose by myself. He had my mother fly to Portland. We drove back to San Jose. My boys slept back in my mother's garage with our dog and cat. I found a realtor and went house-hunting. I found a house I liked on Ridgewood Avenue in the Blossom Hill District of San Jose, bought it, called the van and storage company, and had our furniture delivered. We settled in. My mom and dad stayed with my children in our house; and on June 16, 1966, I flew back to Portland, Oregon, for the commissioning of my husband's ship.

The USS *Patapsco* (AOG-1) was commissioned on June 17, 1966. The next day, I flew back to San Jose. We were back where we had sunshine. The school, not far from us, had a swimming pool. My children were in three different schools. Ronda and Eugene went to Blossom Hill Elementary. Richard went to Dartmouth Junior High. Steven went to Leigh High School. My cousin Maxine lived a few miles from me. My friend Pat Jones lived in my neighborhood. My father wanted Steven to work for him that summer cleaning cars. Dad would pay him a dollar an hour.

Our cat, Herman, had been in a fight. We found him in the flower bed. He passed away that night. We went to the pet store, and Eugene bought two hamsters. He named them Pete and Pat. We didn't know it, but you can't put a male and female together in a cage. The male will kill the female. Now he had one hamster, Pete.

The boys' bedroom on Ridgewood was a nice big room. You could put all three of the beds down single file. Early on Saturday mornings, the children would change their sheets, make sure I had all of their dirty clothes from under the beds, and sweep their bedrooms. One Saturday, we needed cereal. It was Richard's turn to go to the store. He would go two houses down, turn right at the corner, then across the street to Safeway. There was a traffic light at that intersection. After Richard was gone about one and a half hours, Eugene wanted to go get him.

I said, "No, leave him alone."

When Richard finally came home, he said he was reading the back of all of the boxes of cereal to see which one had the best toy in it. He was there so long he got disoriented and couldn't remember where the front door of the store was to get out. Another time, Richard went to the store to get a few bananas. He had a dollar. Bananas were on sale 10¢ a pound. So he bought ten pounds of bananas. He was on Steven's bike and had a hard time getting all of those bananas home.

One Saturday, I had gone to the commissary at Moffett Field to get groceries. Right after I left the house, a lady called and invited Ronda to go with her daughter to a movies. The boys knew it would be okay for her to go, so they helped her get into her new dress and brushed her hair. When I came back from the commissary, the boys told me Ronda was at the movies, and that was fine. Later, when Ronda came home, I noticed they had put her new dress on her backward. It was supposed to button up the back. They had the buttons up the front. She didn't care. She had a good time.

The people next door had a cat, and it had kittens. Herman had passed away. Ronda wanted the little black kitten. I said okay. She named it Missy and put a red collar on it. It slept with Ronda, and it got along fine with Pixie.

Maxine attended the Catholic church not far from our house. On Friday nights, they had bingo. My brother had moved into my neighborhood. My children were older now and didn't need a babysitter. On Friday nights, my sister-in-law, Karen, and I would go to the Catholic church and play bingo with Maxine.

I enjoyed spending time with my cousin Maxine. I was so happy she lived nearby. I would take my children over there for Mexican food. She would bring her children to my house. Maxine's husband, Julian, was from Uvalde, Texas. His parents still lived there. Julian got word that his father was dying. He wanted to go visit his dad. Maxine and Julian had six children—Anita, Junior, Anna, Michael, Mary Ann, and Louis. Maxine asked if I could watch Anita, Anna, and Michael. She said my uncle Mac would take the two youngest, Mary Ann and Louis. Junior would be staying with his uncle and working in the fruit orchard.

I said, "Of course, I would."

That was a long drive. When they arrived in Uvalde, Maxine called to see if everything was okay. It was.

Maxine's oldest son, Junior, had gone to the Santa Clara County Fair with his uncle and a couple of his cousins. When it was time to leave the fair, Junior said he needed to use the restroom. He never came back to them. They searched the fairgrounds. The police were called. About midnight, someone was knocking on my front door. It was the uncle and aunt Junior was supposed to be with. I had never met them before. He told me Junior was missing and he needed to use my phone to let Maxine and Julian know. Julian said he and Maxine would start home the next morning. They left, and everyone went back to bed. I got up early the next morning and went to get my morning paper. Junior was lying on my front porch. He was cold. I brought him in and got him some hot chocolate. I asked him if he wanted breakfast. He said no. He just wanted to sleep. I put him to bed in my room and called Maxine.

I told her, "Junior is here at my house. He is going to stay at my house. You stay in Texas as long as you want."

I'm sure Junior thought he was getting a raw deal. He was working in the fruit orchard while his brother and sisters were going swimming.

I caught a bad cold. My mother came by to check on me. She took the mail out of my mailbox. There were ten envelopes from Carl. I started to open them and found a $100 money order in each envelope. Carl did not want to put them all in one envelope because sometimes bags of mail get lost at sea. He wanted me to have extra money in my checking account in case of an emergency. My mother couldn't wait to get home and tell my dad I had received this money. The next day, my dad showed up and wanted to borrow $500. I tried to explain to him that this was money I might need for emergencies. He promised he would pay me back in a week. I wasn't feeling good, and he wasn't leaving without the money. After a while, I just gave in and wrote him a check for $500. After a couple of weeks, I asked my dad about the money. He said he couldn't pay me back but he had ten acres in Oregon. He would sell me for another $500. My mother said they had driven up there and it was beautiful, a little ponderosa. I wrote Carl and told him what I had done.

He said, "Buy the land. We will never get our money back any other way."

I found out later my father had given the land to my brother. When my dad asked my brother for it back, all my dad said was "Loretta wanted it." Now my brother was mad at me.

March 16, 1967, Carl's ship, the USS *Patapsco*, would be returning to Hawaii. I went to the commissary and loaded the house up with food. My mom and dad would move into my house and watch my children for one week while I flew to Hawaii and met the ship as it returned from Vietnam. My two friends Andrea and Sally had gone to Hawaii when the ship did and lived in navy housing. When they met me at the airport, they placed two orchid leis around my neck, then they took me shopping for a Hawaiian muumuu. That night, the three of us stayed at Sally's apartment and talked for hours. We had a lot of catching up to do. Andrea had booked Carl and I a room at the Holiday Inn, which was halfway between the submarine base where the ship would be docked and Honolulu. They had arranged for a lei made out of multicolored material to be taken out to the ship and put on the bow before it entered the harbor; we wore our muumuus to meet the ship. After the ship was tied up at the dock, we were allowed to go aboard. I got to kiss my husband for the first time in nine months. He had business to take care of before he left the ship. He took me to his office and had the steward bring me ice tea. After he was finished with his paperwork, we rented a car, went out to a nice restaurant, and had dinner.

When we got to our room at the Holiday Inn, the light on the telephone was flashing. Carl had a message. One of the sailors was found dead in his bunk. Black Hand warning notes were found in his locker. NCIS was called. Carl returned to our hotel room about midnight. He would be aboard ship from 8:00 a.m. until noon every day during the three-day investigation. After an autopsy, it was determined he died of natural causes.

Now our vacation could begin. The next morning, Carl wanted to go to the submarine base. They had a big PX.

While there, Carl walked over to the jewelry department and said, "I never bought you a ring. See anything in there that you like?"

I thought he was joking.

I looked down at a three-quarter-carat emerald-cut white gold solitaire and said, "I like that."

He had the lady get it out of the case and said, "It's yours!"

I love my ring. We went to a luau on Waikiki Beach and ate poi and roasted pig. We went to the Polynesian village, had another wonderful meal, and watched them dance. We went to the blowhole where Elvis Pressley filmed the movie *Blue Hawaii*. We went to Fort DeRussy, a beautiful beach owned by the US navy. We lay on the beach, held hands, and listened to the ocean. Anytime I am under stress, I close my eyes and remember that sound, then I am okay. One night over dinner, Carl said his next duty might be a desk job in Saigon.

My week was up, and it was time to return home. While I was gone, Ronda injured her leg while playing around the neighbors' pickup truck. Later Carl would take two weeks' leave and come to San Jose to see the kids. He liked the house I had bought.

One afternoon in June, my phone rang. I answered it, and it was Carl calling from Hawaii. He asked me if I was sitting down, and I said I was. His voice was very sad, and it scared me. He said he had gotten his new orders. My thought was they were for Saigon.

All of a sudden, he yelled, "San Diego! We're going back to San Diego! Go down there and buy us a house."

I replied, "We already have a house in San Diego."

He said, "The children have grown. We need a bigger one."

My mother didn't want me to drive down to San Diego by myself. She said she would come to my house, stay with my children, and babysit my nephew Kenny. My sister-in-law, Karen, would go with me. The children were out of school, and they could help her. It was a long drive. We arrived in San Diego and checked in to a motel, went to a restaurant, and had dinner. The next morning, we got up early and started looking. Carl would be stationed on North Island. I made a circle on my map of San Diego and started house-hunting. There were many new homes being built. I went into one development on Jutland Avenue, north of San Diego. It would be an easy drive for Carl to get to North Island. The houses were Spanish style and ready to move into.

I found one house near the top of the hill—three bedrooms, one and three-quarter bathrooms, a family room between the two-car garage, and the kitchen / dining room. The living room had a fireplace and sliding doors out to the patio. We had another view from the patio, but this time, we were looking east. We saw canyons. The family room off of the garage would be our fourth bedroom. Richard and Eugene would sleep there. They gave me an address to go to, to sign the papers. I had expected to stay in San Diego three or four days, but on the first day, I had found the house and signed the papers.

My sister-in-law, Karen, wanted to go to Tijuana. The next morning, we drove to the border. I left my car on the US side, and we walked into Mexico. We went into the shopping district, and she bought a blouse. She was happy. I drove to my old neighborhood, said hello to Mr. and Mrs. Jacques, then returned to the motel. The next morning, we drove back to San Jose. I made arrangements to get my furniture moved. That didn't take long. A week later, we were living in the new house on Jutland Avenue. Mr. Klint, a realtor in Los Gatos, bought the house on Ridgewood. Now I was not far from where Torrey Pines Military Housing once stood.

The following week, I would go to Lindbergh Field and pick Carl up. He was pleased with the new house. It wasn't far from Torrey Pines Beach. A few months later, we would hear on the TV that the grunion were going to run that night. We invited Roberta, the neighbor across the street, to go with us. We went to Torrey Pines Beach. We were at the right place at the right time. They hit the beach so thick that, when you walked, they came up between your toes. Carl had taken the old toy box to the beach with charcoal, a skillet, and bacon and eggs. He loved to go to the beach and cook. He had just finished eating when the grunion hit the beach. We started grabbing up grunions and putting them in the box. Roberta took some home with her. The children went around to neighbors offering them grunions. A few neighbors took some. We were up all night cleaning fish and putting them in the freezer. They were very good to eat.

Summer of 1968, Carl wanted to take a nice vacation. We planned on being gone a month. He wanted to drive across the southern part of the United States to West Virginia, spend about ten days, and return home driving across the northern part of the United States. He bought a GMC pickup truck with a camper shell. He built benches on either side. The tops opened, and there was lots of storage. I bought foam rubber, cut it to size, and made covers for the benches. First thing to go in the storage area was Grandma Bessie's box, then our sleeping bags and the camp stove. Our animals, Pixie and Missy, will go with us. A neighbor boy next door would babysit Pete.

Stopping at points of interest, we bought a Golden Eagle card; and we had a book with all the camping spots and national parks, KOA camps, etc. Carl installed an intercom between the cab and back of the truck. Now we could talk to each other. The children would take turns riding up front. We drove through San Bernardino, and the first night, we camped on the Mojave Desert in a KOA camp. We could see the lights of Las Vegas. The next day, we visited Boulder Dam. The second night, we camped on the North Rim of the Grand Canyon. We visited the four corners where Arizona, Utah, New Mexico, and Colorado meet, then on to Mesa Verde and saw the adobe ruins. We spent the night in a KOA camp near Walsenburg. The next day, we visited Dodge City, Kansas, and visited Boot Hill on our way to Hutchinson, Kansas. In Hutchinson, we took the children to see the houses we lived in when they were small. We went through Joplin, Missouri, on our way to Clinton, Arkansas, to visit my grandparents

Harrison and Mary Harness. We only intended to visit for a little while, but Grandmother insisted on fixing us dinner. My cousin Vada stopped by with her little girl Dena. Now there were ten people there. Grandmother was fixing one chicken.

I whispered to my children, "Just take a little bit of chicken. We will stop and eat later."

We drove on to Memphis and spent the night on the bank of the Mississippi. There were no camping places. We slept in the truck. The mosquitoes were bad and ate us up. The next morning, after breakfast, Carl dropped me off at a laundry. While I was washing and drying our clothes, he drove the children back and forth over the Mississippi River. We went through Nashville and Knoxville. We pulled off the side of the road near Wytheville. There were no campgrounds. We slept in the truck. Next morning, we headed north to Beckley, West Virginia, near Clifftop, West Virginia. It was Richard's turn to ride up front. Now we were at Nutterville, West Virginia. We spent a week on the farm with Fred and Grandma Lena. Lena hadn't seen the boys since they were babies and had never seen Ronda. We enjoyed our week. Now it was time to head home.

We went through Charleston, West Virginia, and Akron, Ohio, on our way to Elyria, Ohio, to visit Carl's brother Robert; his wife, Marian; and the kids—Susan, the twin boys (Ronald and Donald), and the youngest, Berry. The kids were playing out in the backyard with firecrackers. Richard lit a firecracker. It had a very short fuse, and it went off in his hand, painful but no permanent damage.

It was time to head west. We went through Norwalk, Ohio; Bowling Green, Indiana; Valparaiso, Indiana; Joliet, Illinois; Rockford, Illinois; and Sioux Falls, South Dakota. We drove through the Badlands National Park. On our way to Mount Rushmore, we found a place to camp. The next morning, we went to Mount Rushmore. It was covered in very low hanging clouds. Just before we left, the clouds lifted, and the children said that Snoopy made the clouds go away. We visited Little Bighorn Museum and the monument at Custer's Last Stand. We toured Jewel Cave National Monument. We drove through Billings, Montana, and Gardiner, Montana, and went in the north entrance to Yellowstone State Park. We saw the mud pots, the paint pots, and Old Faithful. We got behind a very slow walking buffalo.

We took the West Yellowstone exit and found a camp outside Pocatello, Idaho, when we camped near bodies of water. The children played in the water. Somewhere in the last day or so, Eugene had gotten into some poison oak. When he got up that morning, his legs were fiery red. We got him to an emergency room in Pocatello, Idaho. They gave him some pills and put lotion on his legs, then gave us prescriptions, which they filled, for him to use on our way home.

Next stop was Craters of the Moon National Monument and Preserve. This was very interesting. We camped in a KOA camp near Mountain Home. There was a fast-moving stream near our campsite. The water was about six feet deep, very sandy on the bottom. The boys saw a beer bottle floating down and started throwing rocks at it. It broke. Carl was upset with them. He didn't want anyone getting hurt later, but he also didn't want them in that deep, fast-moving water trying to get the pieces of glass out.

We were not that far from Brothers, Oregon, and we had time. We decided to go see the ten acres of beautiful trees, the little ponderosa. It was southeast of Bend, Oregon. We stopped at the gas station / grocery store/ post office. We went in and talked to the postmaster. There were no trees. He told us it took forty acres to raise one cow. You had to go down four hundred feet to get water. The only people living there were the road crew who kept the road open in the wintertime.

Next stop was Nevada City, California, to visit Carl's brother Ray and his wife, Georgia. Ray had bought a foundry many years before and moved out of Oakland. We had a nice time there.

We were on the road for over three weeks and had a wonderful time, but now it was time to get home to San Diego.

Steven attended Claremont High School. Richard and Eugene attended Marston Junior High. Ronda attended Louisa May Alcott Grammar School. Early in the year, Ronda's teacher and the principal of Louisa May Alcott came to see us.

Ronda had a very high IQ. They wanted her to go to a school for gifted children. Ronda was in the room with us as we talked. We asked her what she wanted. She wanted to stay where she was. End of discussion.

Ronda's cat, Missy, disappeared. I put an ad in the paper: "Looking for black cat, wearing red collar." We got a couple of calls, but it wasn't Missy. A few days later, Steven was in the canyon behind our house stringing a wire for an antenna for his ham radio and found her body. She had been shot. Ronda was crying. I put Ronda in the car, and we headed for the pound. We were told there had been an outbreak of cat fever and they didn't have any kittens. As we were talking to the lady at the pound, a couple brought a cardboard box with kittens in it. Ronda picked out a long-haired gray kitten. We were told it was a male. She named it Mickey Finn.

Carl and I had gone to the commissary. When we returned home, there was a note on our front door saying my little dog, Pixie, was at the vet a block away and she had been hit by a car. Someone had opened the side gate and let her out of the backyard. The children were at school. The neighbor said she saw a young girl in our yard. Carl ran to the vet's and was told a car had run over her back. She only weighed ten pounds. Her chance of survival was slim. Carl told them to go ahead and put her to sleep. He came back from the vet and gave me the bad news.

Christmas of 1968, my parents came to visit. Ronda now had the canopy bed. They slept in Ronda's room. I made her a pallet on the floor with Richard and Eugene. They were talking about what they thought they were getting for Christmas. The boys were telling Ronda she was getting something to ride. (It's a purple-and-white Schwinn bicycle with a white basket.) The next morning, she was disappointed. She wanted a horse. I told her we couldn't afford to board a horse; but someday, after Daddy retired and we had some land, she would have a horse.

Steven was a ham radio operator. We bought an aluminum shed and put it in the backyard, on the patio. We saw an ad in the paper for a large desk. We bought it for Steve. He spent most of his free time out there.

Richard had a friend, Jon Crabtree. Eugene's friend was Danny Harkelrod. They were all good kids and didn't give me any headaches. Richard and

Jon wanted to order something. They put their order form in an envelope with a couple of dollar bills and some loose change. When the envelope went through the machinery at the post office, it came apart. The boys had to go to the post office and collect their envelope. Richard told me about it. I wrote them out a check, and they reordered the item.

Ronda and the little girl across the street played with Barbie dolls. Ronda had some Barbie dolls with the Barbie chest and lots of clothes, but she was not that interested in them. One day, the little girl came over, and they played with the Barbie dolls. When it was time for the little girl to go home, Ronda gave her all of her Barbie dolls, the chest, and all the clothes. When the little girl got home and told her mother why she had all of these things, the mother called me and told me what happened. I told her that was fine. They were Ronda's dolls, and she could give them away if she wantsed to.

Carl had to fly to Washington DC. He took two weeks' leave and went to visit his mother and his brother Fred. Carl and Fred drove around for a week or so looking for farms for sale. They saw a sign near Nimitz, at the end of a driveway. About a half mile up the driveway, they saw a pink two-story house. There were people around the house. Carl and Fred didn't want to disturb anybody, so they turned the car around and left. A few days later, Carl bought a Beckley newspaper and saw the name of a realtor, Matt Crook. Carl went to Matt's office, and Matt wasn't there at the time. As he was leaving, he saw a man entering the office. He turned around and went back in. It was Matt Crook. Carl asked if he had a listing for a small farm, about fifty acres.

Matt said, "No, but I've got a beautiful three-hundred-acre farm with two houses. Go to Jumping Branch and turn up the Deeds Road. At the end of the road, the farm is on the right. Go look around, and I'll meet you there in about an hour."

Carl went to the farm and looked around. The more he saw, the more he liked. He recognized the pink two-story house as the one he and Fred had seen earlier. Matt gave Carl directions to come in from the opposite side of the property.

Matt arrived and said he was selling this farm for $50,000. Carl told him about the one farm at Elton. Matt knew that property and said he would give Carl $10,000 toward the purchase of this farm. Matt also said he was planning on fixing up the smaller house and, because he didn't get that work done, he would knock off another $4,000. Now Carl felt it was within our reach. They went back to Matt Crook's office, and Carl bought the farm for $36,000. The twostory house was partially furnished. There is a Massey Ferguson tractor in the shed. There were chickens and rabbits.

Carl returned to his mother's house and called me and told me he bought a farm in West Virginia. The house was partially furnished with some machinery, chickens, and rabbits. He told me he was flying home on Friday night and wanted me and the children ready to leave Saturday morning to drive to West Virginia.

"We might have to pay to have our furniture taken to West Virginia, so anything you can live without, sell!"

The children and I started going through the house and moving things onto the front yard. A middle-aged man asked me why we were having a yard sale. I told him my husband just bought a farm in West Virginia. He asked if this house was going to be sold. I told him yes. He asked when my husband would get home. I told him Friday night. He said he would be back Saturday morning to talk to my husband.

Carl came home Friday night. Saturday morning, the man came back and bought the house. Fred called. He told Carl his in-laws were driving from California, bringing his son Tommy to West Virginia to spend a month with him. He normally put them up in a motel and paid for all their meals. He asked if his inlaws could stay on the farm. Carl said yes. Now I had a month before I had to be in West Virginia.

We offered to sell the house on Shady Glade to Mr. and Mrs. Jacques. They said no. They were going on vacation. I put an ad in the paper, listing the house and the ten acres in Oregon, and gave the phone number for the house on Shady Glade. Every morning, I would go to the house. The first day, a man called, came out, and looked at the house. A few days later, he came back and bought the house.

I got a few calls on the ten acres in Oregon, but I explained to them it was high desert. "Took forty acres to raise one cow. You had to go down four hundred feet to get water."

After that, they weren't too interested. One man called, knew exactly where the property was, and wanted it for a hunting camp. I sold it to him for $1,000.

C arl said, "You need a dog. You're going to West Virginia. We have no idea what the neighbors are like. You loved those Australian shepherds. Let's find a kennel where they raise Australian shepherds and get you a new puppy."

We looked in the phone book and found a listing in Mission Valley, and went out to the kennel, they had a litter of four puppies. They were about two months old. I wanted a female. There were two females, one red merle and one blue merle. The red merle was all over the place. She was cute and funny. The blue merle was subdued and quiet. After watching them play around for a while, Carl asked which one I wanted. He was surprised when I chose the blue merle. I told him that puppy needed me. We named her Patapsco Lady, after Carl's ship. The next day, I took her to the vet for her checkup. He found seven foxtails in one ear and ten foxtails in the other ear. After he removed the foxtails, she was as bouncy as the other puppy had been. We also found out she got carsick.

Steven had his learner's permit. I would take him out near the Miramar naval station and let him practice driving.

I took him in for his driving test, and he passed. A few days before we left for West Virginia, his driver's license came in the mail.

We left San Diego early on the morning of July 31, 1969—I; Steven; Richard; Eugene; Ronda; Pat; our dog, Mickey Finn; our cat; and Pete, Eugene's hamster, at Yuma, Arizona. We stopped for gas and got out of our air conditioned car. The heat was brutal. As soon as the cat and dog had a short walk, they were put back in the air-conditioned car. We always stopped at Stuckey's gas stations. With a fill-up, you got a free one-pound box of chocolate candy. Our routine was the following: Ronda took her cat on leash for a short walk. One of the boys took the dog on a leash. They rotated. The other two boys help me carry drinks out in the desert away from a lot of traffic. I let Steven drive. We went through Flagstaff, Arizona, and spent the first night in Gallup, New Mexico. Carl wanted me to call him each night so he would know where we were and that we were okay. The dog got carsick, so we kept her on Milhouse during the day, which made her sleep a lot. After we had dinner and returned to our room at the Red

Roof Inn, they brought in an extra rollaway bed. I didn't get much sleep. The dog had slept all day and was now wide awake. The dog and cat were jumping from bed to bed. They needed their exercise. Steven, Eugene, and Ronda complained about all the noisy trains. I didn't hear it, and Richard slept through it. We got up extra early and drove to Albuquerque, New Mexico, and had breakfast. Richard remembered he had a Spanish omelet. We had lunch in Amarillo, Texas, and probably had dinner east of Oklahoma City. My aunt Thelda lived in Lonoke, Arkansas, just east of Little Rock. I wanted to spend the night with her. It took longer to get to her house. Then I thought we didn't arrive there till around midnight. I called Carl and told him where we were. He was very surprised at how far we had driven that day and gave me strict orders. I was to go no farther than Bristol Jenn. The next night, when I got to the West Virginia line, I had to go over a big mountain. It was too dangerous to do that at night. Years later, there would be two tunnels to make it safer.

We didn't leave Aunt Thelda's house till around lunch. I drove through Memphis, Tennessee. There were no interstates then. You drove through the middle of town. I asked the kids to help me look for road signs to help get through Nashville. They started reading every funny sign they saw, then the car would crack up with laughter, which was not a help.

Finally I said, "The next one who reads a sign that is not a helpful one is going to have duct tape put on their mouth."

(As we were leaving San Diego, Carl had put a roll of duct tape in the glove compartment in case I needed it as a joke.)

I didn't drive very far until Richard said, "Trash can, one-fourth mile."

The car exploded in laughter. But I had to keep my word. I pulled the car over, put duct tape on the mouths of all four kids, and started driving. (Steve would be a senior in high school when school started.) I came to a red light. The kids were laughing behind their duct tape. An older couple pulled up on my left. The elderly lady in the passenger seat did a double take and nudged her husband. He looked, and they both cracked up laughing. They only kept the tape on for a little while. Carl got a big kick out of it when we told him.

We stopped for the night in Bristol, Tennessee. After breakfast the next morning, we went over that mountain to Bluefield, West Virginia, then Princeton.

Carl told me to head for Beckley. "You would see a sign going to the right that would say 'Hinton.'

Take that road until you see a sign that says 'Deed's Dairy Farm.'"

That was the way he went in the first time he saw the farm. Carl came south from Beckley. Now the kids and I were heading north toward Beckley. We saw a sign on the right that said "Hinton." I turned on this road. It took us through Streeter. (There was another road about four miles up that we should have taken.) We were going the long way around. We finally connected to Route 3, which went through Jumping Branch and Nimitz. The "Deed's Dairy Farm" sign had been removed. Carl had told me, if I missed the dairy sign, to continue on and, when the road started downhill, there was a little white house sitting on a bench. That was the other driveway. We drove through Nimitz and started down the hill toward Hinton. I knew something was wrong. I saw a little white house. I went by it three times before I figured out this had to be what Carl meant. But what the heck was a bench? We pulled up the driveway. There were people sitting on the front porch. I asked them if this was the driveway to the old Clarence Deeds farm. They asked if I was Mrs. Amick. I said yes.

They said, "How in the world did you drive from San Diego and find this place?"

I replied, "Believe me, it wasn't easy."

Later Carl would tell me he had used their phone and told them he had bought the farm and his family would be driving from San Diego.

August 3, 1969, we were home. This was the last move I would have to make. We started up the half-mile driveway to the house. It was a nice drive. At the top of the hill, it opened into beautiful fields. Now I knew why Carl fell in love with it, and there stood the two-story pink house. You could see it before you got to it. I love old houses. This one was built in 1914. It had four bedrooms. Fred's in-laws were still here. After we looked around a little bit, we headed for Hickory Flats to spend the night with Fred and Grandma Lena. This gave Opie and Nettie time to get their things together. We would return to our house the next day. It was a wonderful feeling knowing I would never have to move again. Carl got orders to Washington DC and made arrangements for our furniture to be shipped. The kids and I would be on the farm by ourselves for about six weeks. Carl took a month's leave before he had to report to Washington DC. Carl would retire from the navy after twenty-two and a half years on October 1, 1970.

Ronda got her horse, a little Appaloosa named Cody.

ABOUT THE AUTHOR

Loretta was born in San Jose, California. Raised in Campbell, California, she cut the apricots and picked the prunes until she was old enough to work at the Hunt's fruit cannery in Campbell. She met this cute sailor from West Virginia while he was stationed at Moffett Field. She had no idea what the Lord had in store for her.